THE COLD, COLD HAND

*More Stories of Ghosts and Haunts
from the Appalachian Foothills*

THE COLD, COLD HAND

More Stories of Ghosts and Haunts from the Appalachian Foothills

James V. Burchill, Linda J. Crider,
and Peggy Kendrick

RUTLEDGE HILL PRESS®
Nashville, Tennessee
A Thomas Nelson Company

Published by Rutledge Hill Press, a Thomas Nelson Company, P.O. Box 141000, Nashville, Tennessee 37214.

Typography by E. T. Lowe, Nashville, Tennessee

Library of Congress Cataloging-in-Publication Data

The cold, cold hand : more stories of ghosts and haunts from the
  Appalachian foothills / [edited by] James V. Burchill, Linda J. Crider,
  and Peggy Kendrick.
    p. cm.
  ISBN 1-55853-543-8
  1. Ghosts—Appalachian Region. 2. Haunted houses—Appalachian
  Region, I. Burchill, James V., 1930–   . II. Crider, Linda J.,
  1947–   . III. Kendrick, Peggy, 1963–
  BF1472.U6C647 1997
  733.1'09758'2—dc21   97-25332
                                                CIP

Printed in the United States of America
5 6 7 8 — 05 04 03 02

Dedicated to the storytellers of folklore and legend in appreciation of their efforts to preserve our heritage and pass on a sense of history so revered in these mountains, the home of our hearts.

CONTENTS

Acknowledgments,   9
Prologue,   11

Aunt Mary's Stories,   15
The House Where Bea Lived,   19
Tales from Childhood,   24
The Visitors,   27
The Swami,   31
The Bridge,   34
The Curse,   37
Clinic Ghost,   42
Birds,   46
Pikeville Haunts,   52
Cemetery Visions,   55
The Witch,   57
Mountain Spirits,   59
Angel Wings,   63
Specters from Another World,   64
Blackfoot's Ghost,   67
Coming Home,   72
Memories,   75
The Man in the Yellow Slicker,   77

The Dancing Sprite, *80*
The Return, *82*
Hangman's Rope, *84*
The Cold, Cold Hand, *86*
Resident Ghost, *91*
Footsteps in the Night, *95*
Panther, *97*
Premonitions, *101*
Letting Go, *104*
Reminders, *106*
Grace, *109*
Spring Place, *113*
Mule Mountain, *116*
Ghost at the Lake, *119*
Virginia's Ghost, *123*
Séance, *125*
The Man Who Hated Flowers, *128*
Courtship, *130*
Alice's Friend, *134*
The Shadowman, *138*
Mother Morehill, *141*
Traveling Man, *144*
Jack, *146*
The Road Less Traveled, *149*
Dreams, *151*
Boardwalk, *156*
The Hermit's Wing, *159*
Josie's Ghost, *162*
Perfume and Footsteps, *165*
Billy's Revenge, *169*
Red Clay Bank, *173*
Dove, *176*
The Purple Cloud, *179*
The Keepers of the White Dog, *182*
The Old Innes Place, *185*
Epilogue, *189*

ACKNOWLEDGMENTS

SOME NAMES OF PLACES AND PERSONS have been changed in this collection of short stories revolving around the foothills of southern Appalachia.

Special thanks to the following persons for their help in making this book possible.

Billy Bernhardt
Doug Swanson
Jonathan Young
Billy and Mary Teems
James and Sandy Nelson
Jodi and Barbara Waters
Brannon Holt
Kris Kelly
Virginia Webb
Kay and Lloyd Davis
Bea Stewart
Mitchell and Tonya Jones
Don Crider Family
Ruth Jones and Family
(the late) Richard H. Waters

Ruth Roberts
Melodie Loyd
Daisy Greer
Stacie Young
Marie and Louise Stamey
River Street Girls
Daddy and Mama
Herbert, LouAnn, and Paula Teague
Tony and Charlotte Withrow

Prologue

Spirits roam the appalachian foot-hills just as surely as do their stories and legends, many of which are as old as time itself. We, the authors of this book, know without doubt that they are there, some-where beyond our sight and hearing. And, like so many others, we have been touched by their presence.

It was a warm autumn day in October 1993. Jim Burchill, Peggy Kendrick, and I, Linda Crider, were adding the finishing touches to our first book, *Ghosts and Haunts from the Appalachian Foothills.* We had met at my house, located on top of one of those venerable foothills.

A gentle breeze sang through the trees, causing the kaleidoscope-colored leaves to dance and drift softly to the ground. We marveled at the beauty surrounding us and, after exchanging pleasantries, went to work.

Leaving windows and doors open to take advantage of the last bit of warm weather, we spread out the pages of our manuscript in the living room and kitchen. Time passed quickly, and by the time we had finished with the last story, night had fallen. We were pleased with our ac-complishment, knowing that a part of our heritage was secure in the written words.

With the manuscript in Jim's custody, we walked onto the porch to say our good-byes. As the last "good night" rang out in the now chilling darkness, Peggy gasped, clutching her hands to her chest.

"My truck!" she wailed. "Where is my truck?"

"What?" Jim and I asked in unison, looking into the driveway for the little yellow pickup.

"Where's my truck?" Peggy gasped again in disbelief.

"I don't know," said Jim. "Are you sure you drove?"

"You know I did—I parked right there!" the young woman shouted, pointing toward the vacant expanse beside the porch.

"That's right," I added, recalling Peggy's arrival for out meeting.

"So, where is it now?" she bellowed, waving her arms in dismay. "It couldn't just disappear without leaving any sign."

"Well," said Jim softly, almost in a whisper, "I think it has."

Looking through the darkness, I was bewildered and silent. It couldn't simply vanish—not really—not something as big as a truck.

The three of us had not been more than fifteen feet from the vehicle all afternoon and evening. Only a wall with open windows and a bit of space had separated us from the pickup. We had heard nothing, seen nothing, and now there was nothing where Peggy's truck had been.

A sudden chill wind rustled the spidery needles of nearby pine trees, and the night seemed to close in on us. My vision was drawn down the long, narrow, twisting driveway. Through the trees, about one hundred yards away, something loomed in the darkness.

"There," I said, pointing a shaky finger. "I think it's over there."

Peggy, Jim, and I hurried through the night down the

driveway to the place I had indicated, and there sat Peggy's truck. Its wheels were pointed straight, the hand brake was pulled, and the transmission was in gear. The pickup completely blocked the driveway, and there were no scratches or dents anywhere on it.

It took some work to jockey the truck around and head it in the right direction, but within half an hour, Peggy was on her way home and Jim left shortly thereafter.

There was no way Peggy's truck could have made the trip down the driveway without making a sound or sustaining at least some sort of damage. But it did.

It was quite a while before we could speak of the incident, believing that the spirits of the Appalachian foothills either didn't like our book and were trying to stop it from being published, or that they indeed liked the stories and didn't want them to be forgotten. We prefer to believe the latter and hope to appease any anger we may have stirred with this second collection.

Our first book, *Ghosts and Haunts from the Appalachian Foothills*, has been used as a teaching tool. It has captured the minds of not only adults but school-age children, furthering their interests in folklore and legends.

We have gathered and written this second collection of strange legends and stories of the Appalachian foothills in the hope that they will spark readers' imaginations for many generations to come.

AUNT MARY'S STORIES

BILLY BERNHARDT'S ANCESTRAL ROOTS are buried deep in the Appalachian Mountains. The heritage of folklore and legend is a treasure and legacy he shared. Billy sat in his office chair, head back and eyes closed, remembering his childhood and the old stories he had first heard during those years. Two of those old tales in particular stood foremost in his mind. Both involved his family, the events having touched those he loved.

Billy opened his eyes, sat up straight in the chair, and in a soft, low-pitched voice began to recount the stories that had been related to him by his aunt, Mary Bramlett.

My Aunt Mary always told the family stories. She told a lot of others, too, but it was the family ones she was most interested in. Maybe she wanted us kids to know them and pass them on to our own children.

They were a history of sorts, reminding us perhaps that life isn't always good, but is often hard and painful, strange and haunting—and sometimes unbelievable. That's especially true for those of us living here in the north Georgia mountains of Gilmer County.

15

Some of Aunt Mary's stories used to scare us kids so bad, we'd be afraid to go to bed at night. But the two she told most, she always swore were true.

Aunt Mary lived out in the Yukon section of the country in a big old rambling two-story house. Many years before, a rich man had lived there, and everybody for miles around suspected that he'd hidden a fortune in gold somewhere in the house.

One night, some men came to rob the man, who was a pretty big fellow and more than likely put up a good fight. When the robbers couldn't make the man tell where he had hidden his fortune, they killed him, cut off his head, and then ransacked the house until they found the gold. Undoubtedly, the robbers became scared because of what they'd done. They had to know that they would be hung if they were caught with the stolen gold, so they hid it. The robbers probably decided it would be better to let things calm down a bit and then come back later to get the gold they'd killed for. After all, they were the only ones who knew where it was hidden.

It was shortly after the murder that Aunt Mary and her husband, Monroe, moved into the old house. And on that first night—and every night thereafter—some very strange things happened.

When Aunt Mary and Monroe went to bed, the front door would swing open and a man's heavy footsteps could be heard echoing across the wooden floor toward the rocking chair in front of the living room fireplace. The chair would creak as a headless figure dressed in a long overcoat and high-topped leather boots settled into it and slowly began rocking back and forth. That headless man would continue to rock until someone got out of bed and lit the lamp, and then he'd disappear. He never bothered anything—he just came into the house every night, sat by the fireplace, and rocked.

16

The headless man was seen by a lot of Aunt Mary's neighbors. He always wore the same high-topped boots and long overcoat, and many people thought he might be searching for his lost gold as he walked the roads and fields.

One morning, after several years of the haunting, Aunt Mary went to fetch water from the spring. When she got there, she noticed that great holes had been gouged in the moss-covered ground around the spring—almost as if someone had been frantically searching for something. After that day, no one—not Aunt Mary or anyone else living in the area—ever saw the headless man again.

Maybe he'd been standing guard over his gold all those years, or maybe he was waiting for his killers to return. No one knows for sure. The gold was never found and the murderers were never caught.

* * *

The other story Aunt Mary always told took place in our family, too.

It was in the summer, sometime back in the 1920s, and Great-uncle Joe was in his early teens. He was playing with an antique pistol, pointing it every which way and pulling the trigger, like kids will do. After all, the gun was probably broken and didn't have any bullets in it anyway, so it made a good toy.

Cousin Everet was just a small child, and that day he was playing in the yard with an old rooster, which was his pet. Everet was tossing pebbles at the bird as it scratched in the dirt, when Joe suddenly turned around and pointed the pistol at the rooster.

"I'm going kill that rooster," Joe said, teasing the little boy.

Everet fell to the ground, grabbed the bird, and clutched it to his chest. " No!" he screamed. "You can't kill my rooster."

Joe still had the gun aimed at the pet, but this time when he pulled the trigger, the gun fired—but it was Everet, not the rooster, who lay dead.

Joe had pulled that trigger a hundred times or more that day, and the only sound had been the hammer snapping down on the empty chamber. But in a flash, the pistol had come alive and taken the life of a young child.

Everet's body was laid out at my grandfather's house, and the extended family all came to sit with the body. That was the way things were done back then—a body wasn't left by itself, and the immediate family wasn't left to mourn their loss alone.

Late that first night, Aunt Martha and Aunt Lorie had to go to the outhouse. As they stepped outside, both of my aunts saw a white lamb standing in the yard. Aunt Martha walked up to the lamb and reached out to touch it, but before her hand could reach its soft white head, it disappeared.

Nobody knows where the ghost lamb came from, why it was in the yard, or how it managed to vanish. But many things that take place here in these mountains don't have explanations. Folks just accept them as they are and go on with life and living as best they can.

THE HOUSE
WHERE BEA LIVED

BEA AND KAY ARE SISTERS, BUT MORE than that, they have been best friends for a lifetime. They've shared childhood dreams and adult realities. They've experienced life and death and all the in-betweens on the borderline of Georgia, Tennessee, and North Carolina in the Appalachian foothills of their ancestors.

They tell stories of times past, places abandoned, and things perhaps best remembered only in whispered tones.

Bea sat in her chair in the living room, gazing about the room with clear blue eyes. Kay sat across from Bea as if to give her sister encouragement.

Bea ran fingers through her short, dark hair and began to speak in a low voice.

The house where me and Ed, my husband, was living in East Town sold, and we had to move. There was a little house up on the river a piece that had been empty for a while, so that was where we were going to. We knew

a killing had took place there, but that didn't have anything to do with us.

Dally Weaver, a neighbor woman, came by one day
before we left and reminded us that a boy had been killed
by his uncle in that house. She was real upset, saying
there was still blood all over the walls and the floor. She
didn't want us to go there, but I told her we had to move
somewhere, for the house we was in had sold and that
was the only place we knew about.

Dally just shook her head and said, "I'd set my things
on fire and just walk away before I'd live in that house."

Well, we moved on up there, and sure enough, there
was bloodstains all over the walls and floors where that
man, in a drunken fit, had killed his nephew. I cleaned
and cleaned, but it didn't matter what I did, I couldn't get
that blood gone. We just tried not to think about what
had happened and didn't mention it, either.

When we got our belongings moved in, it wasn't long
before strange things started happening.

Mrs. Prince, a woman we'd known for a long time,
and her two girls came to stay the night. Her man had got
drunk and run her off. We just had two beds, and I told
her they'd all have to sleep in the same bed. She agreed
that would be fine, saying she just needed a place to stay
till her husband sobered up and let them come home.

We lit the lamps and sat up and visited for a while,
then as the night got along, we all went to bed. The lamp
globes hadn't even got cold when Mrs. Prince began
screaming. She just screamed and screamed, "I'm smothering! I'm smothering! I'm smothering to death!"

She was in such a state, we all got up and stayed up
the rest of the night. By the next day her husband
sobered, and she went home believing her husband's
drunken meanness wasn't near as bad as spending another night in our house.

One Saturday night, right before the big gospel singing convention, Uncle Horace came to stay overnight at our house. Dad was there, too, so I told Uncle Horace he'd have to sleep on the cot-like bed I had pushed up against the wall by the window in the front room.

Uncle Horace was a gentle person and never complained about much of anything. He was always welcome at our house and would have been satisfied with a pallet on the floor. After a short visit to catch up on the health and goings-on of the other seldom-seen family members and acquaintances, we said our good-nights, dubbed the lamps, and went to bed.

The next morning as we all sat down at the table for breakfast, Uncle Horace said, "I'll tell you right now, I'd lay out in the woods in a storm or anywhere else for that matter before I'd sleep in this house again."

That tickled Dad, and he laughed and asked why.

Uncle Horace answered, "Lord, them chains went in and out and over that window all night long."

The cot had been pushed up against the wall where so much of the boy's blood was. That could have been the place where he fell, or maybe he tried to get out the window or something. Anyway, Uncle Horace never came back to spend the night as long as we stayed there.

Then one day I was ironing. I ironed in the kitchen, which was in the back of the house. That's where the cookstove was, and I always heated a flatiron on the cookstove top. There wasn't electric irons at the time, and besides, we didn't have any electricity. I had just got started good when I heard my brother, Claude, call me by name, clear as a bell from the front porch. I called out and said I'd be right there. I'd left the front door locked. I went to the door, opened it, and seen nobody was there. I figured he'd walked around to the back, so I went out and walked around, too, but he wasn't there. Nobody was.

People always left pickles and jelly and stuff like that on the table because there wasn't refrigerators and we didn't have a springhouse. One night, just after we went to bed, a terrible noise sounded from the kitchen. It was loud and crashing, and I was sure the table had fell or broke and all the jars on top had fell to the floor and busted.

Kay was staying with us then, and she heard it, too. Kay was always scared when she was there. She'd wrap up all over with the quilts, even her head, no matter the weather, when she went to bed. When the crashing sounded, Kay screamed just like she was dying. Lord, but she was scared nearly to death.

I told Ed to get up and light the lamp, that I was sure the table had fell. When we all went to look, there was nothing amiss. Everything was just as we left it before we went to bed.

Some nights after we'd go to bed it would sound like somebody was in the loft taking on just awful. The sounds were so pitiful, so moaning. I can't explain how painful they sounded. Folks said it was the spirit of the boy that got killed, or maybe the spirit of the man that killed him.

Lots of times we'd set on the porch and hear footsteps inside. They'd echo in every room. When we'd go in to see if anybody was there, the stepping sounds would stop and we wouldn't find anybody.

Another night we had company. It was Mr. Holden, who lived way out in the country. It was already late when he came by our house on his way home, so we just asked him if he wanted to stay and leave out early the next day. He agreed that was probably the best thing since a bad storm was coming up.

The haunting noises were so bad and so loud that night that nobody dared go to bed. And when daylight came, Mr. Holden left and I made plans to move from that terrible place. It was storming awful, but I had already decided I'd not spend another night in that terrible, terrible house.

There was a little house, nearly in town, that was empty. The owner rented it to us, promising there were no spirits living there.

The storm didn't let up that day, but we moved anyway, leaving behind that house with its bloodstained walls and floors and sounds of death and dying. We had lived there two or three months, and after we left, nobody ever lived there again. After a few years it just kinda died and fell in on itself. I felt better then, knowing it was gone. But I still remember it all. I guess those memories . . . well, I don't guess they'll ever be gone.

TALES FROM CHILDHOOD

"*I* *WISH I COULD REMEMBER ALL THE* *stories Dad and Grandpa and Uncle Horace used to tell us kids,*" *said Kay Davis, Bea's sister. "They knew so much about these old mountains, the people, and their ways. They knew the old haunt stories, even experienced a few. But too much time has passed, and I can't recall much about them now.*"

Kay shifted her position on the sofa and sighed. The expression on her delicate face, framed by soft gray curls, appeared to transcend time, and she smiled. "I remember a couple of the stories now. They were two, I guess, that maybe I heard the most. I can almost hear Grandpa and Uncle Horace telling them."

Seems that when Grandpa was a young man, folks rode mules or horses or in wagons to get to where they was going. There weren't any cars or roads, just rutted wagon paths and trails. But the folks living here in the mountains went to church any way they could. They knew, down deep, that the good Lord was their strength when they'd run out themselves.

There were several churches scattered about the mountain settlements, with different denominations and preachers. Of course, I think people just went to whatever church was having services. They didn't usually overlap one another, so everybody could go to every meeting. It wasn't just a Christian duty to go to church but a way of socializing, politicking, and keeping up with what was going on in the world outside our own homes.

It's strange how churches so many times are associated with strange tales, but both the stories etched in my mind happened close to churches up on the east side of the county. Bea, too, will tell you these stories are true. We both heard them near all our lives, and I'm sure they was both told for truth because Grandpa and Uncle Horace would never lie, especially to us kids.

Grandpa and his folks lived way up on Big Creek when he was growing up. He and Great-aunt Liz had been in the field hoeing corn one summer day, and when dinnertime come, they left their work and headed home to eat.

They were coming up the hill from the field and had just got up to the road when they saw two children walking down the road toward them.

Aunt Liz asked who they were, and Grandpa named over some of the neighboring kids. Grandpa kept watching, and the children kept coming closer to them. The children were holding hands.

Grandpa called out to them, but they didn't answer. The children got closer and then turned and walked up into the cemetery.

Aunt Liz stopped dead still, staring at the children, and Grandpa only took a couple more steps, then he halted in his tracks.

"Do you see them kids?" he asked his sister. "They don't have any heads!"

Aunt Liz gasped and shook her head in agreement.

They didn't move, just stood and watched as the children disappeared among the gravestones.

They never could explain what they saw that day, but I remember Grandpa talked about how bad it bothered him for a long time after that, and I could see the worry lines etched in his face every time he told the story.

* * *

There was another story Uncle Horace told lots of times. It happened at Macedonia Church, down the road a piece from where we lived and grew up. He told this story and swore it was the truth.

There was a big old oak tree growing alongside the road near the church. Uncle Horace said that one night Jeb Willis was riding by on his horse, making his way home, when that tree bowed way down low and lit up real bright and spoke. It said, "Come here. Come here."

The tree spoke real loud and spooked Jeb and his horse, too. Old Jeb yelled and the horse started to run off. It took nearly a mile before the horse slowed down enough for Jeb to take control.

Jeb didn't go back that way but took the long way around, not getting home till the middle of the night.

Nobody ever mentioned anything like that happening again. But it always made me wonder if that tree was haunted or if maybe it happened more times than that once and nobody ever spoke about it.

You know, if people told stories like that now, they'd be laughed at. But we sure heard them when we was kids. Folks would sit around and tell about strange happenings and us kids would listen. They was all good people, too. I believe all them stories was true.

THE VISITORS

ELISE NO LONGER SLEPT IN HER BED. SHE found it difficult to rest there. Her mattress was too soft, the quilts were too heavy, and getting out of bed seemed to require more effort every morning. So now Elise slept in her recliner in front of the television. That seemed more practical, considering the cost of washing clothes. Elise simply wore her dress all night, then changed clothes in the morning when her visiting nurse came to help her take a bath and make breakfast.

Some mornings the nurse's knocking on the door woke Elise, but she usually was awake long before the nurse arrived. She even managed to fix her own breakfast if it wasn't too cold or too hot and her joints didn't ache.

Though she was ninety-four, Elise still had some pride left.

She'd taken care of her own home just fine for seventy years. She washed, cleaned, cooked, raised children, and kept a garden and a cow most of her life, only giving those things up when her body began to fail her. It was what her mother had done, what her grandmother had done, and what just about every other woman in the southern Appalachians had done for hundreds of years.

Now Elise spent most of her days sitting in the recliner with a lap quilt of her own making tucked around her legs to fight the chill that never quite seemed to leave her body. She watched television and talked on the telephone and looked out her window at the few cars that passed. Once in a while a visitor came, usually one of her relations come to bring food or ask about some bit of family history.

One cool October morning, a Saturday, Elise sat dozing in the recliner. She had dreamed all night and woke more exhausted than when she went to sleep. Taking a little nap before the nurse came wouldn't hurt a thing. Besides, she was an old woman and had earned the right to do whatever she wanted.

A knock at her door woke Elise. Drowsily, she opened her eyes and called to the person to come in. Most anyone who knew her would come in and save Elise the effort of getting out of her chair and walking across the room. But this visitor kept knocking.

Her mouth set in a grim line and her watery blue eyes blazing, Elise pushed the raised footrest down with the heels of her bare feet and reached for her cane. Grumbling, she slipped on her house shoes, then slowly stood. The visitor never stopped knocking.

For a moment Elise simply stood still. She had to gauge whether or not her head would get swimmy, making a walk across the tiny living room a danger. Everything seemed fine, so she made the seven-foot journey from her recliner to the front door.

"I'm coming," Elise said in irritation. Her voice was weak, and her throat felt ticklish from not having talked that morning. Her words were not very loud, but she assumed anyone at the front door could hear her since it wasn't that far away. But the visitor kept knocking.

"If I didn't know better . . ." Elise muttered under her breath, but she did not complete the thought, for it was ridiculous.

Grasping the cold doorknob, Elise would have liked nothing better than to throw the door open and glare at the annoying person on the other side, but she was afraid the movement would cause her to fall down. It still surprised Elise how feeble her body had become with age, how the simplest things had to be carefully planned.

The knocking stopped abruptly, and for a moment Elise wondered whether or not she had imagined it. Sometimes she heard the telephone ring, and when she picked it up, no one was on the other end. Of course, that could have been because she didn't get to the telephone fast enough. Perhaps she hadn't gotten to the door fast enough, either.

With an exclamation of disgust fresh on her lips, Elise opened the door, half expecting no one to be on her front steps. People can get so impatient with an old woman. It's hardly fair, she thought, and then all such thoughts fled her head.

"Sisters," she said, her voice barely above a whisper. "What are you doing here?"

Two women stood on the steps. Both were dressed in their Sunday clothes, complete with black straw hats done up with rosebuds hand sewn from silk ribbon. Elise stared at them a long while, and they looked back at her, their mouths drawn up into smiles.

"It's been years," Elise said, and both women nodded. "But why are you here?"

They continued to smile, but the smiles were fading. In fact, everything about them was fading: their features, their ankle-length dresses, their black lace-up boots, and their black straw hats with the hand-sewn rosebuds. And then Elise found herself alone, standing in the open doorway with a chill wind blowing across her bare legs.

As quickly as she could, she closed her door. An hour later the nurse arrived, and Elise told the surprised woman about her visitors. The nurse asked Elise if she couldn't have mistaken the two women for someone else. Perhaps they were only people selling books or magazines.

"I know my own sisters, all right," Elise said. "Didn't I make those rosebuds for their hats my own self? I did. But that was over seventy years ago. That was before Martha died of the influenza and Sally died in childbirth. No, they've come to warn me that it's almost my time to go."

The nurse was terribly sad, but Elise seemed pleased.

THE SWAMI

WHEN SIXTEEN-YEAR-OLD CINDY WON THE local writing contest, Mary Willard said, "We were as happy as could be. After Cindy and her friends left, Mama and I settled down to a cup of coffee."

"You know, Mary," began Mama, "I won a writing contest back in 1956."

"You did? I never knew that. Why didn't you tell me?"

"I never told anybody about it," the older woman sighed.

"Why not, Mama?"

" 'Cause something happened. Something I or my friends didn't understand. I still don't really understand it . . . it was strange."

And with that, Mama began to tell her unusual tale.

Nobody was more surprised than I was when I won the writing contest. The contest was run by the Electric Power Company, with each local company picking a winner. First prize was a three-day weekend at the state capital. Each winner could pick someone to go with them. I chose my cousin Martha.

We were sure excited. Our first train ride, a tour of the capital, and we stayed at a fancy hotel.

Sunday afternoon we had some free time, and Agnes, a winner from the southern part of the state, suggested we stroll around the city. Agnes's friend Florence joined us, and it seemed we walked for miles.

"Oh, look down there!" cried Florence. "It's a street carnival. Let's go!"

So we went and it was fun. Just as we were leaving, Martha noticed a fortune-teller's tent, which we entered, giggling.

A man entered from the back of the dark tent, smiled, and said, "Madame Zambi will read your fortune for a quarter each, or for a dollar and a half you can have a séance."

"Let's get the séance," said Agnes. "I'll pay."

Madame Zambi came in and sat down at a small round table, and the four of us joined her, forming a circle. Madame wore a turban with a large red stone in the center. "That's a ruby," whispered Martha.

Madame wrapped her gaily colored gown around herself and said, "Everyone hold hands. Now if we make contact with the other side, only one at a time ask a question." With that, Madame Zambi closed her eyes and began chanting in what sounded like a foreign language.

We all giggled, and Agnes hushed us. I looked at Martha, and we both tried our darnedest to stop laughing. Then a man's voice came from Madame Zambi's mouth, the voice of a young man.

"Where . . . where are you?" asked Florence.

"I am on the other side," answered the young man.

Martha, looking pale, asked, "How long have you been on the other side?"

"I'm not sure," said the man's voice coming from the fortune-teller.

Agnes asked, "How old are you or were you?"

"In my twenties, about twenty-four when I came over."

Now it was my turn. Martha's hand gripped me so hard my hand was white.

"Who were you? What was your name before you crossed over?"

"I was an actor. My name was James Dean."

"Oh, bosh!" said Agnes, breaking loose and standing up. "This is a fake. James Dean is still alive."

Martha said, "Look at Madame Zambi." The seer, her face paler than Martha's, if that was possible, was shaking her head. Finally, she got control of herself and said, "I'm sorry it didn't work out. Here is your money back."

All the way back to the hotel we laughed and jeered about what a fake the Madame had turned out to be.

At six o'clock we left the state capital. Daddy met us when we arrrived at the train station and home we went.

Later that night, after all the excitement of the contest and the trip, I couldn't get to sleep. I turned on my small bedside radio. The news was on. A chill went through me as the newscaster said: "And actor James Dean died last night in an automobile accident near Paso Robles, California. Dean was born in 1931 and died September 30, 1956. He had just finished filming the movie *Giant.* He was twenty-four."

I'll never forget that night. And Martha and me, well, we never told anyone about Madame Zambi and James Dean—until I just told you.

THE BRIDGE

THE SUN SETS EARLY IN THE MOUNTAINS of Fannin County, Georgia, located where the borders of Georgia, Tennessee, and North Carolina come together. The view is spectacular as the last bit of day's light touches the trees in all their skyline splendor.

Fair and her daughter-in-law, Lydia, were passing through the area on their way home to an adjoining county after visiting a family member in the hospital.

Lydia drove the narrow roads, so common to the region, and the two women talked casually about everyday things. It had been a pleasant drive, and they had been pleased with the patient's recovery.

The sun slipped behind the mountains and night quickly descended. The highway stretched before the women like a long, twisting black snake. They were alone on the dark stretch of road, and an eerie feeling began to descend upon the travelers.

As they rounded a curve, a concrete bridge came into view. A woman dressed in a long, white, flowing gown was caught in the car's headlights. Her skin was as pale as her gown, and her hair was long and black as a raven's wing. She stood at the side railing of the bridge, leaning over and reaching out beyond her.

She gave no notice to the oncoming car. Fair and Lydia, both shocked to see a lone person in the dark night, were somewhat awestruck. There was no time to stop, no time to see if the woman needed assistance until they had passed by.

"Did you see that woman?" asked Fair.

"Yes," answered her daughter-in-law as she checked the rearview mirror. "Do we need to . . . she's gone! She's not there now!"

"Are you sure we saw someone?" Fair asked, turning to look back into the empty night.

The woman wasn't there. Maybe she never had been, the women decided, believing that the long day was perhaps playing tricks on their imaginations.

A few years later, Fair and her sister, Mary, were driving along the same stretch of road in the black of night. An eerie feeling again began to shroud the travelers, and the mountains crowded close as Mary continued down the twisting road. Just as they rounded a curve, the car's headlights caught sight of a man dressed in the clothing of a long-ago era hanging over the railing of the same bridge.

"What was that?" asked Mary.

"A man," answered Fair.

"Well, should we stop?"

A chill swept through both women as they looked back to find nothing but the night covering the bridge. The man was gone.

Seeing an access road that led to a nearby town, Mary made a fast turn. The women were shaking in fear when they saw a sheriff's deputy, flagged him down, and in trembling voices urged him to investigate whatever it was they had just witnessed.

The officer tried to calm the nearly hysterical women.

"Follow us," Mary said. "The man was dead or something, just hanging there on the bridge railing."

"And the woman . . . I saw a woman there a few years ago at the same place," said Fair in a shaky voice.

"What?" Mary gasped.

"I didn't want to scare you," Fair replied.

"We have to go now," said Mary, returning her attention to the officer standing beside the car.

"I know the place," said the uniformed man, who quickly got into his car and drove off with lights flashing and siren blaring. The women followed, and the three soon came to the spot where Mary and Fair had seen the man.

A brief investigation proved the area to be empty. There was no man on or around the bridge or in the cavern below.

The women shivered with a chill that went deeper than the night warranted.

"This isn't the first time I've come to this place to check out someone seeing what you did," said the officer. "It happens a lot. We want to believe maybe it's just kids playing pranks."

"How long has this been going on?" asked Fair.

"A little more than thirty years now," came the answer. "That's as far back as I can recall."

THE CURSE

I HAVE BEEN A FREE-LANCE WRITER FOR several years. I write about unusual things, like the strange and eerie happenings that sometimes occur in the foothills of southern Appalachia.

I had heard of the Swayzee curse but really didn't know much about it, only that it supposedly was responsible for cutting down the Swayzee men and women in the prime of their lives.

John Swayzee was the last of the line. He was married but left no children when he died in an automobile accident at the age of thirty-six.

After John's funeral I spent several days trying to find out about the curse. I learned nothing and finally decided to see John's widow, who lived on a hill in the large, well-kept antebellum-style house that Edward Swayzee had built some sixty years ago.

"I never heard of any curse," she said. "But I did hear John's older brother died young in a horrible accident, just like John did in the car wreck."

I spent a couple more days asking around the small North Carolina mountain town but discovered nothing of any importance. I then packed up and drove home to Fannin County, Georgia.

It was there that I ran into Aunt Maybelle and, after catching up on family matters, asked what she knew of the Swayzee curse. Aunt Maybelle thought for a moment, then said, "Go see Joe Hamen. He is the only one left that would remember what it was all about. He's about ninety now. I guess he's still alive."

I followed Aunt Maybelle's directions and drove farther back into the Appalachian Mountains than I ever had before. I parked the car next to a mailbox stating "Box 212, Joe Hamen." I walked up a gravel path to an old but well-kept cabin, and sitting on its small porch in a rocking chair was an ancient man. A large dog lying next to him eyed me warily.

The man saw me, laughed, and asked, "You the fellow who wants to know about the Swayzee curse?"

"Why, yes," I answered. "But how did you know?"

He laughed again and said, "This isn't the North Pole, you know. I have electricity and a telephone. Besides, your aunt Maybelle called. Said you'd be up to see me. Have a seat."

Joe Hamen, by all accounts, was ninety-four years old. His eyes were rheumy, and his hair was sparse on his pink scalp. Oh, but his mind was sharp, and his memories of those long-ago times staggered my imagination.

"Edward Swayzee was a con man and a crook," Joe began. "It happened, oh, back about 1930 or so. Where the Swayzee mansion sits now was the property of Wilber and Hanna Baker. They'd been married for sixty years when times started to go bad. They managed a small vegetable garden and some chickens, but that was about it. The Great Depression really hurt folks around here."

Joe lit his pipe, patted his dog, and got a faraway look in his eyes. "The Bakers owned their property outright and had two hundred dollars in the mattress for taxes and emergencies. One day Edward Swayzee rode up to the Bakers' house and the Bakers invited him in.

"Now the way it was told back then, Swayzee was soliciting partners for a vacation hotel and resort he was going to build in these mountains," Joe said as a hard look crossed his face. "For a small investment local folks could get first dibs on a chance to get rich. Swayzee said if he didn't get enough local money, he'd get city bankers to invest and the profits would leave the area. Both the Bakers believed him, so except for the tax money, they gave him the rest of their money.

"A year went by and Wilber got sick. I guess he got pneumonia. They took him to the county seat, where in them days they had a small hospital. In fact, it was in the doctor's house. Wilber died, and with burial expenses Hanna was broke. She used the tax money to live on, and when the taxes came due, Hanna couldn't pay them.

"Swayzee's resort company filed for bankruptcy. Of course, Swayzee never lost a dime. It was all poor locals who were hurt.

"It wasn't long before there was a tax sale. Swayzee insisted on it. Since the politicians were in his pocket, he got the Bakers' place at the courthouse steps.

"Hanna Baker was dying when the sheriff went to evict her. She passed away with the sheriff and the deputy right there. She screamed her last words, and I'll tell you, son, everyone in the valley heard them. They seemed to echo and bounce around these old mountains for what seemed an eternity. I heard them myself, and I got a chill, I'll tell you.

"She didn't say much. She just screamed, 'I curse you and all the crooked Swayzee men and women, and I curse all the future Swayzee breadwinners. None will ever see their dreams come true.'"

Joe paused to relight his pipe, smiled like an impish boy, and then continued.

"Edward Swayzee built that mansion on the Bakers' property, and the day he moved in, he tripped over a paint can one of the painters had left. He crashed down the stairs and broke his neck. Edward had two sons. The oldest drowned just as he was about to open a new department store. He was thirty-seven. The youngest was twenty-nine when he hung himself. Folks said the curse got to him."

"Were there any more tragedies?" I asked.

"Yes, John Swayzee's father had two brothers, and they both died in horrible accidents. And John's father, at the age of thirty-nine, cut his leg with a chain saw and bled to death before help arrived. John's brother Earl—he was a little older than John—got shot in a hunting accident. And that is the end of the Swayzees."

"Do you believe in the curse?" I asked Joe Hamen when he finished.

"No, not really," he answered. "But you give me your address, and if what I think is going to happen does, I'll get in touch with you."

About six months later I received a letter from Aunt Maybelle. Inside was another sealed envelope with my name on it. Aunt Maybelle's letter stated that three things had happened. First, John Swayzee's widow moved away up North somewhere. Second, the Swayzee mansion burned to the ground. The sheriff suspects arson but hasn't any clues. Third, Joe Hamen passed away and left a letter addressed to me.

I opened the letter and could tell by the faint handwriting that it indeed was from Joe. The letter read:

> You asked me if the Swayzee curse was real. I said no, I was waiting for something to happen. Well, I lied. I was waiting for the final act—the burning down of the Swayzee mansion. Yes, I lied. I believed in the curse with all my heart and soul. I wanted the curse to come true. You see, what folks around here didn't know—or didn't remember—was that Hanna Baker was my aunt. Her maiden name was Hanna Hamen. And if on

occasion in the past I helped the curse along, so be it.
But believe it, the curse was real.

I Go Now in Peace
Joe Hamen

CLINIC GHOST

MANY OF THE BUILDINGS IN AND AROUND the Appalachian foothills have stood for more than a century. One such structure was located in the southeastern reaches of the mountain chain at the intersection of five roads. It was originally built as a general store/trading post, and its owner and his family lived in the back. Over the years the building served well the people who lived and conducted their business there.

In 1995, the building was slated for demolition. The cities were reaching out with interstate systems, and the old structure with its uneven floors and added-on rooms was unworthy of being saved. One of its last residents told of strange happenings that had occurred within its walls.

"The old building saw a lot," said Richard Waters, D.V.M. "Babes born, old folks die, and all the troubles and satisfactions of life in between. There was even a wedding in one of the bedrooms."

He laughed and scratched his head, recalling when his veterinary practice was housed there.

"I don't know when I or any of my employees first noticed the . . . the . . . I don't know exactly what to call them, except maybe ghosts or spirits," he continued. "But there was more than one.

"Everything was always being moved, and the kennel doors were always opening and closing. But for whatever reasons, each of us thought the other was doing it, so it continued for quite a while before anything was said. As a matter of fact, it wasn't until Julie, one of the workers, began to talk to an unseen person that we all realized we weren't seeing everything that was taking place around us.

"Julie was the youngest and maybe the most receptive. She would busy herself with whatever task was at hand and then find herself answering someone behind her. She assumed it was one of the other women working there, but when she chanced to look, she always found herself alone.

"As time passed, things continued to be moved, Julie still talked to someone unseen when she was busy, and a feeling of being watched hovered around us.

"We asked everyone who might know about the clinic's past but didn't find any tragic history. But we did talk to a few people who believed the place was haunted.

"We laughed it off and often joked about our 'resident ghost,' but it wasn't always funny. It was pretty scary to be there alone in the wee hours of the night."

Once, when all the employees had left early due to holiday plans, Dr. Waters's teenage daughter, Jodi, was called in to assist with emergency surgery for a dog that had been hit by a car.

"The clinic always had cold spots here and there, and it was strange to step into them," Jodi said. "But they were at least ten degrees colder throughout the building that day.

"The hall had one, there was another in the lounge, and there were also two in the main lobby. And in the operating room, as we performed the surgery, one occurred instantly where I stood. The hair on my neck prickled and stood up. Goose bumps came up on my arms, and some kind of strange icy coldness ran through me.

"Before I could catch my breath, Dad felt someone tap him on the shoulder. He turned his head and asked, 'What?' but there wasn't anyone there—at least there wasn't anyone we could see."

No one knew exactly how many ghosts or spirits inhabited the building, but there were two for certain. One was believed to be a child. Its gender was never known, but it was often heard running from room to room and down the hallway, laughing.

The other was an old woman. The doctor and his employees concluded that she was the one who talked to Julie. Perhaps she had been a tidy person and was responsible for finding a place for everything left lying about.

Dr. Waters said that many times while he was working late, his car keys would be gone when he was ready to leave. After much searching, he would find them in strange places, such as under the sink or in the towel drawer.

Once, after staying very late to keep watch on a seriously ill animal, Dr. Waters was preparing to leave when he heard keys jangling, the back door open and then slam shut, and the kennel doors banging against their steel frames. He looked on his desk, and there before him lay his keys. He quickly checked the door, which was closed and dead-bolt locked. He noticed that the building's cold spots were icy and heard a child's footsteps and laughter echoing about all the rooms.

Dr. Waters said he didn't stay to search for answers after checking the back door and the status of the sick animal but instead hurried out of the old building and nearly ran to his car, which was parked in a nearby lot.

"The hairs on my neck stood out and my skin was crawling," he said matter-of-factly. "I know that if I had turned and looked back, I would have seen the old woman standing at the window. I could feel her. She was watching me."

BIRDS

SOME CULTURES BELIEVE BIRDS DELIVER our souls to heaven and that without them, we would languish on this earth, lost and wandering.

In the southern Appalachians there are many legends concerning birds. For instance, many believe it is bad luck for a chimney swift, or any bird for that matter, to fly into one's house. Or, if the birds go to roost early in the day, a storm is on the way. And if a bird flies in your window . . .

Ellen was a widow of many months. She was raising two sons and a daughter on her own. Many times she found herself sitting at the dining room table, having a cup of coffee, and looking out into the backyard. At those times she often thought of her late husband.

Sean and Ellen were often at odds during the last few months of his life. He was dying of cancer and wanted to make amends for the way he had treated his family and friends. Like an alcoholic apologizing for the past, Sean spent hours talking on the telephone and writing letters to people he felt he had wronged. He even invited people to the house just to say he was sorry. But in all that time he never said he was sorry for all the things he had done to Ellen.

Ellen could easily recall the way she felt about Sean just before he died. She was hurt and resentful. The morning before he died they argued over some ridiculous letter he wanted to send to a boy he had bullied in grade school.

"For all you know," Ellen said to Sean as he waited for her to write his words on the clean white sheet of stationery, "this guy doesn't even remember you. Why should he care whether you apologize to him or not?"

"I care," Sean said, and though he looked weak and tired from the disease ravaging his body, his eyes were still bright with purpose.

"Why?" Ellen demanded. "Do you think this is going to get you into heaven, Sean? Because if you do, I've got news for you. The people you should be saying you're sorry to are right here in this house. But it's probably too late for that anyway, so you should just forget it. Forget everything!" Sean died late that afternoon, and Ellen still felt sadness in her heart.

One morning, before the children woke and started their noise, Ellen was sitting at the dining room table, looking out at the backyard and wondering if her words might have been like some sort of curse, a curse that was holding Sean's soul back from heaven. That's when the bird bumped into the window.

Ellen barely saw the bird coming. It was hardly a flutter of wings before its tiny brown body rattled the pane of glass. And then it was gone, and Ellen remembered what her grandmother had said about a bird flying into the window of a house of mourning. This, Granny Findley had said, was a sign that the newly departed had a message for someone left behind. But what, Ellen wondered, is Sean trying to tell me?

She gave the matter little thought the first time, reasoning that it was just a clumsy sparrow that had been confused by the clear pane of glass. The next morning when it happened again, she was not so sure. By the time the bird had bumped into her window the third consecutive morning, Ellen was considering the possibilities more carefully.

"Is Sean trying to tell me that he is all right—that he's going to or is already in heaven?" she wondered. "Or is he trying to say he lost his way?" The last thought gave Ellen no comfort at all, and for hours on end she brooded over it. Finally, she began to concentrate on the first thing she had thought of: Sean was fine and had made his way to paradise.

On thinking of her husband only in a positive light, Ellen became convinced that she was right—and for her own piece of mind, she had to be. Surely that was what Sean was trying to tell her.

On the fourth morning the bird did not come, and Ellen's guilt began to melt away. She felt that Sean had been forgiven by everyone and could go on to the next life. He'd just been waiting for her to forgive him.

*   *   *

Maggie's father, Rick, died in the winter, and by spring she missed him even more than she had months earlier. He was far too young to die, she was too young to be without a father, and it seemed awfully unfair.

Maggie threw herself into her work and tried to fill up the hours between morning and sleep so she would not have to dwell on her sorrow.

One morning, just as dawn was pinking the sky, Maggie sat at her desk writing a story for her writers' class. The windows of her bedroom were open, the blinds up, and the curtains thrown back. It was a very cool morning, and the air was so fresh and crisp that Maggie preferred it to the warmth of the rest of the house.

Her mother, Deana, sat at the kitchen table reading the newspaper, and except for the rustling of the paper and the scratching of Maggie's pen, the world seemed a silent place. Suddenly, that tranquillity was rent by the shrill cry of a whippoorwill.

Startled, Maggie looked toward the window facing the backyard, and though she could not see it, there in a juniper bush sat a whippoorwill, crying his song for all he was worth. Maggie had heard these birds before, but they had never been so near the house.

"Do you hear that?" she called to her mother.

"Where is it?" her mother called back.

"I think he's in the bush outside my window."

Maggie had once read that the natives of southern Appalachia thought whippoorwills were actually the souls of relatives and friends who had recently departed. Wanting to believe this was true, Maggie embraced the legend, and from that morning on, she hardly missed her father anymore. After all, she felt him near her every time a whippoorwill called.

* * *

On an April morning five years after Maggie first heard the whippoorwill in the juniper bush outside her window, her mother joined her father in death. Following a long illness, Deana finally weakened and died. When Maggie walked into the house later that day, she felt something different in the atmosphere of the home she had shared with her parents for so long. She knew the spirit of her father, Rick, was no longer there with her.

There had been times when she just knew her father was in the house. Sounds, a heaviness to the air, a certain comforting feeling that she found difficult to express—all were testament to the presence of Rick's lingering spirit.

Later Maggie would think her father's spirit stayed around after his death because he had not expected to die first. He always talked of what he would do when Deana died, not what she would do if he died first. So when Deana died, Rick felt he could finally go on. Maggie knew that as well as she knew her own name.

The morning after her mother died, Maggie rose early. She liked to have a few hours of quiet before dealing with the real world. She drank a cup of coffee, ate breakfast, and tended to a few things around the house she suddenly found herself alone in. Presently, she went outside, and that's when she saw the gray-brown dove on the railing of the deck.

The dove was calling to another of its kind, and that dove was answering in the same plaintive cry. The first turned its head toward Maggie as she stepped out onto the deck and then slowly took to wing in that curious, ruffling way mourning doves have. The dove flew about twenty feet and landed on the low branch of a pine, settling in next to its mate. Maggie thought little of it that morning.

The next morning Maggie rose early again. She knew she had to make the house ready for relatives who would be coming from far away for Deana's memorial service. Part of her chores was to clean out the refrigerator, a hateful job at the best of times. Maggie almost welcomed the normal activity and soon found herself with a pot full of scrap food, which she carried out beyond the shed and dumped onto the ground for the raccoons and possums.

As she straightened from her task, Maggie saw two gray-brown doves sitting on the limb of a tree. For what seemed a long while the birds simply sat there as if unconcerned about Maggie being so close. Finally, they flew away and Maggie began to wonder.

On the third morning Maggie thought little of the doves. She had a guest to feed and a long day ahead of her. That night, at seven, everyone would gather in the Methodist church to say good-bye to her mother. It was a moment she had thought about often during her mother's many hospital stays, but now that it was upon her, she felt she was not ready.

As she stepped out onto the smaller of the two decks to see what sort of day the family would have, at least weatherwise, she heard the doves at the foot of the steps. And as usual, they did not seem startled by her presence.

When she looked over the railing, she saw the pair of doves at the bottom of the steps. Taking their time, they walked about a bit and then flew away. Maggie never saw them again, but she believes they were trying to tell her something.

Maggie believes that the doves were the souls of her parents and had lingered on this earth just long enough to let her know that they were finally together again, that everything was all right, and that they are waiting for doves to guide Maggie and her sisters and brother to heaven.

PIKEVILLE HAUNTS

MELODIE LOYD RELATES SOME STRANGE tales told to her by her grandfather, Sam Akers.

Sam Akers as a teenager was a young blood, always ready to do battle and most times winning. Growing up in the coal country of Pikeville, Kentucky, a fellow better be tough.

One night young Sam was walking down the railroad tracks, heading to his aunt's house to meet his cousins and drink a little moonshine. When those lads drank shine, they meant business.

Sam wasn't far from his aunt's house when he heard a growl behind him. He kept walking. Then he heard heavy breathing and a loud groaning noise. Turning around, Sam saw a large hairy beast coming toward him. At first he thought it was a bear and bent down and picked up two rocks. That was when Sam noticed the hairy beast wasn't walking; it was floating over the tracks.

"God Almighty!" screamed Sam. "It doesn't have any legs!"

Sam's heart pounded, and his breathing stopped as he thought, "Hell has come to get me!"

The beast bore down on Sam, groaning and breathing with a roar that Sam surely thought could wake the dead. The creature went right past, or through, or around him. Sam was never sure which.

Sam ran to his aunt's home in a panic and frantically told his cousins about the beast. They got a lantern and went looking for whatever had scared Sam, but there was no sign of the hairy beast or anything else that could have caused such fear in the young man.

From that day on Sam was a changed man, for he was no longer a boy. He never drank moonshine again or any other liquor. Sam started going to church, and he became a pillar of the community and one of the town fathers.

"It was a sign for me to change my ways," Sam would say whenever he spoke of that night. "That hairy beast was a warning to me—and I heeded it."

*   *   *

There was a church-school in Sam Akers's hometown of Pikeville. The building also was used for town meetings and other groups' get-togethers.

On the morning of an important meeting that most of the townfolk would attend, Sam woke up and declared, "I'm not going to that meeting tonight."

When asked why, Sam replied, "Something terrible is going to happen there, and I want no part of it. I had a dream last night, and it warned me not to go."

No matter what his family or friends said, Sam was adamant. He would not go to the meeting, and that was final.

Sam was right. The meeting erupted into a fight and shots were fired. Two men were killed and several were hurt.

School was canceled the next day while the women of the church tried to clean up the blood. But as much as they scoured, they couldn't get it all.

The next day the children went back to school, and about midmorning it began to rain. Soon the students and teacher heard a knocking sound coming from under the floor.

"It's one of the town boys under there with a broom handle," the teacher said. But when she went outside and looked under the building, no one was there.

After that, every time it rained the knocking sound could be heard. It even happened during Sunday services, but when the church elders searched for the cause, they too found nothing.

One night, Sam and his family were going to the movie theater in town. It was raining, and just as they passed the church-school, the knocking began. Sam checked the building and found no one there. But every time Sam took a step, something inside also took a step, and every time Sam made a sound, whatever was inside made the same sound. There was no rhyme or reason for the knocking sound, but it was there.

The old building is gone now, and only the old-timers remember the church-school, the shootings, and the knocking sound that occurred whenever it rained.

CEMETERY VISIONS

TONYA JONES KNOWS OF THE HAUNTING tales rumbling about the Appalachian foothills, for she has heard them all her life, both from older generations and the present one. Her husband, Mitchell, also knows of the unexplained mysteries that take place in the hills and hollows, for he has experienced their strangeness on occasion.

"It happened to Mitchell," said Tonya, her eyes wide with the telling. Her long, curly brown hair caught the sun's rays as she turned her head from the legal papers in front of her. "I know it's true."

She gazed across the room as if maybe the story was best left untold, best left in the cemetery and the tidal pools of silent memory.

It was in the summertime, and Mitchell and some of his friends were out on the east side of the county. They were just riding around, enjoying the day. He said it was sunny and warm, not a cloud in the sky, when they rode by the old Tickanetly church cemetery.

It's way out in the country, and there would generally be nobody there. But this day there was. Mitchell said there was a woman in a long red dress and a child wearing blue.

The dresses were from another era. And they stood as if grieving beside a weatherworn gravestone.

Mitchell stopped the car, and he and his friends watched as a cloudlike shadow formed and rose up behind the two. It grew until it consumed the woman and child, then all was gone. Everything just vanished, as if it had never been there at all.

The men, being brave, young, or foolish, ventured over to the place where the apparition had appeared, but they found nothing, not even footprints in the dusty red-clay soil surrounding the grave. But each knew he had indeed seen something there and began searching among the gravestones.

Mitchell said the stones marking the graves where the two had stood were old and timeworn, but the names were still legible. A woman and her child, both of whom had died in the late 1800s, lay beneath the earth of the old cemetery, and someone still grieved.

Mitchell was disturbed by what he had seen and told the story to a friend, who went to the county library and searched the records to find the story among the archives.

A woman and child bearing the same names as those on the gravestones had been savagely murdered by the woman's husband. It was also recorded that the husband was a brutal man who had always abused his family.

The account in the archives was so detailed that even the burial clothes of the murdered mother and child were described. The woman wore a long red dress and the child was dressed in blue.

THE WITCH

KALEB PALMER, A YOUNG MAN IN HIS twenties, tells stories his family has experienced through the generations. He knows well the adventure of searching out answers to the unexplained, for he has walked the haunted foothills, looking for solutions.

Supposedly there were practicing witches here a long time ago. I never saw any real witches, that I know of, but there is one buried up in Fannin County. There on Aska Road, in the cemetery. I've seen the place.

The gravestone is old and stained, and moss grows on the back side of it. I don't rightly remember the witch woman's name, but it's carved into the stone marker. And down below her name, it says "I Shall Return."

That right there, her saying she will return, always gives me the creeps when I pass that old cemetery. Makes me wonder if right then might be the time she was referring to.

My aunt lives in Fannin County. She says the legend of the witch has been around for a long time. According to the stories, maybe she's already come back.

My aunt told me that if you walk around the witch's headstone three times with your hand placed on top, and call her name, the spirit will come. It will stay beside you as long as you are in the cemetery, but when you step beyond its bounds, the spirit disappears.

My aunt did this and says it's very true. I've never walked around the stone like that. I've wanted to try it a bunch of times, but then I think, "What if this witch is just waiting for the right person to call her name?"

She's locked in the cemetery somehow, and for whatever reason, she can't leave. Not yet anyway.

MOUNTAIN SPIRITS

MOST PLACES AROUND THE APPALACHIANS have areas that are truly eerie, and many people consider these places to be haunted by evil spirits. The stories may vary from one person to another, but certainly each has strange tales to tell upon his or her return from those locations.

One such place is known as Elf House. Located in the foothills, the building was abandoned by its owner one night for reasons unknown to the local folks. Elf House has been uninhabited for years, yet its foreboding presence draws adventure seekers who are daring enough to face the unknown spirits that haunt these old hollers and hills.

Mary Teems and her family live in the heart of Gilmer County, Georgia. They've been in these mountains for generations, and telling the region's old stories and legends is a long-standing family tradition.

During one night's storytelling, Sandy, Mary's daughter, spoke of nearby locations that held uneasy feelings or perhaps restless spirits.

"The worst place, I guess, for me," she began, "was Elf House. Every teenager for miles around has probably been there looking for ghosts, spirits, haunts, or adventure. There's something there. I don't know what, but I felt it."

The room became silent as each person looked at the other.

"What happened?" asked Mary, wondering if maybe it would be best if she did not know; but as a mother with two small boys still at home, she needed to.

Sandy said that years before, she and some friends made the drive to the infamous, reportedly haunted house. When they got out of the car, an eeriness shrouded the group. They trekked up the old driveway, overgrown with briers and brambles, toward the old clapboard house, which was falling down amid a patch of tall grass and weeds. The eeriness grew in intensity, almost gaining substance as it crowded in on the youngsters.

As the group scrambled through the weeds, they discovered a path about two feet wide that circled the house. It was clear of grass, weeds, rocks, and everything else except the heaviness of a cold, icy warning that seemed to emanate from something supernatural.

The young people quickly retraced their steps, and as they drove away, a black car with tinted windows appeared from nowhere and began to follow them. It made no sound and stirred no dust on the dry red-clay road. The car followed closely until the teens reached the main road, and then it disappeared as mysteriously as it had appeared, leaving the youngsters to wonder where the ghost car had come from, where it had gone, and, more importantly, why it had followed them.

"It's a place best left alone," said Sandy. "The cold there goes deeper than any chill I've ever felt, and I won't go back there. One warning to stay away is enough for me."

*   *   *

James, Sandy's husband, said that he, too, had made a visit to Elf House in his teenage years. Seems it was a rite of passage for the young men of the area. Curious, youthful bravado took them there. But it was total fear of something beyond the realm of understanding that caused them to flee the place where spirits dwell and strange stories are born.

James and a few of his friends had heard the strange tales and haunting stories for years and one night decided they would see for themselves if Elf House held anything supernatural. The road was rutted and weather-worn after the boys turned off the main road, and their car bounced and scraped bottom as they drove along the narrow road twisting through the rural reaches of the Appalachian foothills.

A small white house, long abandoned and dilapidated, sat on the left-hand side of the road. The yard, overgrown with high weeds and sapling pines, boasted a sagging, empty clothesline that swayed in the slight breeze.

The boys laughed as one of the group remarked that Elf House's ghosts had even scared off the neighbors. They parked the car and walked the rest of the way to the abandoned house, which had once belonged to a retired doctor who moved to the mountains to become a writer. As they prowled through the rooms, they yelled for any spooks to make their presence known but were met only with silence.

Then someone saw an ax hanging over a door. Each of the boys tried to remove the ax from the wall but to no avail. Not even the strongest of the group could budge it. A chill fell over the boys, and fear ran rampant as they rushed to be gone from the strange, suddenly cold place.

James said a black truck began to follow them down the drive as they ran toward their car. Fear gripped the boys like a heavy hand as they scrambled inside and sped back down the rough road, the driver paying little heed as the underside of the vehicle scraped across the humps and bumps.

But when they passed by the dilapidated old house, said James, "Clothes, newly washed, hung on the clothesline. Only a few minutes before, they weren't there, and the hair on my neck stood up when I saw them. And the old black truck—I don't know where it came from, but it was there. And then, when we reached the main road, it was gone. I couldn't hear a sound coming from the truck, but it was bearing down fast on us as we ran like some kind of demon was chasing us.

"I guess I had to go, just like the rest of the folks who do," James said of his visit to Elf House. "But it's a bad place, holding something unnatural, and I'm one of a whole bunch who won't be going back."

ANGEL WINGS

FAMILY TIES, RELIGION, LIFE, AND DEATH are regarded as one entity here in the low-lying mountains of Appalachia. Some are said to be blessed—or cursed—with a sense of knowing when their time to pass from this life will come. No one knows where this ability comes from, and perhaps there simply is no explanation.

It was about fifty years ago that Myrtle sat on the front porch of her mountain home, stringing beans for supper. She watched as her children busied themselves in the yard, playing tag and hide-and-seek amid squeals of laughter. Their childhood games filled the warm autumn day.

Her son, Clay, was the youngest and most imaginative. He loved to watch the birds soar high overhead and had even learned to identify several of their distinct calls.

Clay left his siblings in the yard and came to stand in front of his mother. "Mama," he said, smiling, "I'm going to be an angel and fly like the birds. And I'm going to watch over my brothers and sisters."

A few days later Clay became ill and died. But his mother found solace in believing that her son had become an angel that now soared high above and watched over his family.

SPECTERS FROM ANOTHER WORLD

"I GUESS IT COULD HAVE BEEN A DREAM," said Ann, a wife, mother, and teacher in the Appalachian foothills, as we talked about stories for this book. "But if I was dreaming, it seemed like a very real dream at the time."

"I don't know if you remember," she continued, looking me straight in the eyes as if she expected me not to believe her and wanted to catch me at it. "It was a Saturday. February, I think. Anyway, Mama was giving our cousin's wife a baby shower, so I guess this was about twenty-five years ago, 1971 or thereabouts."

I nodded. I could recall the tiny pieces of iced cake, barely two inches square, and the pink and yellow and green mints and salty nuts. The women played games. It occurred to me that women don't play games at baby or bridal showers anymore. A lot of things are different now.

"I ate lots of nuts and mints and cake that evening, so much that I almost made myself sick," Ann said. "See, that could explain it all away if it was a dream. All the food could have made me dream it all."

"But you don't think it was a dream," I said. Ann didn't answer. She just looked at me and went on with her story.

"That night after I went to bed, I didn't have any trouble getting to sleep. And I don't remember dreaming, at least not until I heard the noise outside.

"My bedroom faced the backyard. Beyond the yard was a little bank, and at the foot of the bank was a field our neighbor always planted in peas. A thin line of trees separated the field from a hay field. On three sides of the field grew pine trees. In that field is where I saw it."

"Saw what?" I asked.

"The UFO."

My stomach clinched and I got that familiar tingle I always get when someone is telling a particularly interesting or unusual story. "Go on," I prompted. "You saw a UFO. . . ."

Ann nodded, still deadly serious. "I got out of bed because I heard this high-pitched hum. The UFO rose from the field and turned its belly toward me. The humming noise wasn't like a helicopter or airplane. And then it slipped back down behind the trees. I knew immediately what it was."

"What did you do?" I asked, thrilled by the account and wondering why things like this never happened to me.

"I ran into my parents' room," Ann said, not betraying herself by showing amusement. Obviously the incident still frightened her. "I woke them up and told them what I'd seen, but they didn't believe in things like that and told me I was only dreaming.

"I was just trying to warn them and they didn't believe me. I was trying to save my family from being killed by aliens, and my parents weren't even going to help me. So I went back to bed and pulled the covers over my head.

65

"I was cold and clammy, heart racing scared. I was afraid we were going to be killed. But I guess I wore myself out because I finally went to sleep.

"The next day, Sunday, we all went to church and then out to eat. It was cold that day, but later I went out and caught my pony anyway. I rode him for a while, then I couldn't help myself—I had to go to the place where I'd seen the UFO rise up.

"I rode through the pulpwood yard that bordered the field, then crossed the field itself. When I got to the far end I saw it, the reason why I'm not at all sure I was dreaming."

I held my breath and her serious expression never wavered. "What did you see?" I asked, my voice barely a whisper.

"The grass in the field was bent down in a circle as if something very heavy had rested on it. It was in the exact spot where I saw the UFO land."

There are some who might argue that stories about UFOs don't belong in a book about ghosts, but things such as UFOs and aliens haunt our landscape just as surely as specters wearing Confederate uniforms. Who is to say we are not seeing visitors from other planets when we think we're seeing ghosts?

BLACKFOOT'S GHOST

In THE LITTLE COMMUNITY OF HOLLY Hills, nestled against the low-lying mountains of Appalachia, most folks have always kept animals, for work as well as companionship.

The Henry family, not having much land and with the father working a public job, had no need of larger animals such as horses, mules, or cows. Over the years they acquired a few cats and a dog or two that were either given to them by neighbors or just appeared at some time and stayed, knowing their duties would be few. The cats were mousers, and the dogs were responsible for varmint control and also for greeting family friends and warning of strangers to the small house.

The dogs were of no particular breed but were large in size and loud of voice. The Henrys were quite proud of their mongrel dogs and praised them often for doing such a good job.

The cats, too, were of mixed breed and color. They appeared to enjoy catching mice that scurried in from nearby fields and woods, seeking shelter in the snug, cozy home with its tight-fitting windows and doors and underpinnings all the way around.

A specialty of the Henry house was the glass door

leading out onto a wide front porch. It allowed the animals to watch their human family before and after their work was finished. Apparently it created an even stronger bond as the folks inside could also see their animals.

It was a warm spring day when a silver tabby appeared at the glass door with a mouse in his mouth. Mrs. Henry saw the cat and went to investigate. When she opened the door, the cat laid the dead mouse at her feet and sat down as if awaiting her response.

The woman, appreciating the gesture, smiled and said, "Good boy. I guess this proves we need another cat around here. You can stay."

The cat meowed as if understanding the woman, picked up the mouse, and scampered off the porch. The woman went back inside to continue her daily chores, telling her daughter, Brie, about the strange newcomer and what it had done.

Brie hurried to find the silver-colored tabby, but after searching the yard, barn, and even the garden, was unable to find it.

The next morning, Brie was the first to see the cat with strange yellow eyes and shiny fur sitting outside the glass door. When she opened the door and stepped onto the porch, the cat came close and laid a dead mouse at her feet.

"Good kitty," Brie said, reaching to pat the smooth head. She was a bit cautious, not knowing the cat's temperament. But the silver tabby warmed to the little girl, raising itself to meet her outstretched hand. Brie picked the cat up in her arms and nuzzled it lovingly. It was then that she discovered the coal-black pads on the bottoms of the animal's feet.

"I'll call you, Blackfoot," Brie said, returning the cat to the floor of the porch.

Again the cat meowed as if understanding what the girl had said. It was a deep, roaring, growling kind of meow, and Brie stepped back warily. The cat eyed her with suspicion, then retrieved the dead mouse and scurried off the porch.

Brie hurried inside to tell her mother that she, too, had seen the cat, held it, discovered its black-bottomed feet, and named it Blackfoot. She also mentioned the mouse the cat had brought.

"It's a good cat that can provide for itself," Mrs. Henry said. "Some cats are lazy and depend on people to feed them, and I guess those cats would starve around here with the dogs eating what few scraps there are."

Blackfoot became a permanent member of the Henry animal family, even though he didn't socialize with Pie, Ringtail, or Fluffy, the other cats, and definitely had nothing to do with Spot or Blackie, the dogs.

Each morning Blackfoot would appear at the glass door, wait for someone to come and speak to him, and then drop a newly killed mouse at the person's feet. After a few words or a pat on the head, the cat would pick up the mouse and disappear until the next day.

The daily ritual continued for many months, until one day Blackfoot didn't come, nor did he appear for the next week or so. Brie looked everywhere for the silver tabby, calling as she searched, but was unable to find it.

Then, on a very cold and rainy Sunday morning, Mrs. Henry saw the cat outside the door. She could tell something was wrong and hurried to investigate before Brie woke up. Blackfoot's coat was dirty and matted. Wounds caked with dried blood crisscrossed his stomach and one eye was swollen shut. He tried to meow but was too weak to make much of a sound at all.

Mrs. Henry called her husband, who took the cat out to the barn. They didn't tell Brie, knowing she would be very upset that Blackfoot was so ill.

Mr. Henry checked on the cat several times during the day, and by nightfall it was determined that it would be kinder to destroy the animal and end his suffering. Brie wasn't told, and after she went to bed that night, Mr. Henry took care of the deed and disposed of the cat's body.

The next morning a mouse was found outside the glass door, and Brie became excited, believing that Blackfoot had returned. She called and called after the cat, but when the tabby failed to appear, she finally gave up her search.

The next morning another dead mouse was found outside the glass door. This continued for a week or more and was very strange indeed, said Mrs. Henry.

One night Brie awoke and, being very thirsty, made her way to the kitchen. She saw two soot-black paws pressed against the glass door, as if Blackfoot were standing on his hind legs and bracing himself against the door with his front feet in order to peer inside.

Brie hurried to the door, but when she reached it, only Ringtail, the oldest of the cats, was there. Ringtail yowled long and loud when the little girl opened the door.

The next night the entire family saw a reflection of what appeared to be Blackfoot in the glass door as the parents were taking Brie off to bed. It was gone in an instant, and again Ringtail yowled.

Later that night Mr. Henry saw a cat he would have sworn was Blackfoot sitting on the porch banister. Knowing that it just couldn't be the silver tabby, he went outside to investigate. He found nothing there but heard Ringtail yowling hauntingly in the dark night. The next morning another dead mouse was found outside the door.

As time passed, the dead mice appeared less often, and sometimes days went by without any sightings of the cat or his gifts. Eventually, the mice were all but forgotten, and Ringtail's yowling finally stopped.

It's been years since the black-footed cat first appeared at the Henry house, and Brie is now grown. Her parents finally told her of Blackfoot's end, but Brie says she still occasionally finds a dead mouse lying just outside the glass door on the wide front porch.

COMING HOME

"OH, IT'S JUST SO BEAUTIFUL HERE," SAID Barbara Lowe.

"Yes," agreed Jane Kramer, "I guess it's about the nicest cemetery in the county."

"You know," said Don, Jane's older brother, "it was our grandmother's grandmother who picked this spot out. She bullied and harassed the deacons until they finally agreed to put the church cemetery here. And that was over a hundred years ago, back in the 1880s."

The East Side Baptist Church cemetery stood high on a hill overlooking the small town of Hardeston, the county seat. It was the most beautiful and best-kept cemetery in an area that featured many pristine and serene graveyards.

The visitors were college students—the girls were sophomores and Don was a senior—and would be returning to school in three weeks. All were dressed in jeans and were cleaning off the family plots, pausing now and then to appreciate the area's beauty.

"Let's take a break and walk around," said Don. "I'll show you some graves and headstones that go back to the last century. Granny Putnum took me through a couple of years ago. There is a lot of our county's history here."

72

"Yes," said Barbara, "I have some kinfolk up near the top."

It was just before dusk and the trio strolled through the graveyard. There were no clouds in the sky as the sun began to slip behind the Appalachian foothills.

"Look at these gravestones," said Barbara. "Some of these headstones date back to the 1800s."

"Some of these graves aren't as well kept as the others," said Jane.

"Why are they allowed to run down?" asked Barbara.

"Well, a lot of these families died off and some left the area," Don answered. "Next weekend the pastor has a group of the younger members of the church who are going to clean off these older graves."

The three sauntered along, reading off the names and dates on the tombstones, although some were so weather-worn that their inscriptions were illegible.

As they reached the top of the hill and started down the other side, Jane exclaimed, "Wow, all of the sudden I'm freezing!"

"Yes," shivered Barbara, "I'm cold, too; it must be the wind."

"There doesn't seem to be any wind, but it sure got cold," said Don.

The chill settled on the college students as they walked between the headstones.

"Gee, it's getting colder by the minute," said Don.

"Look," whispered Barbara, "over by that oak tree."

"Which oak tree?" asked Jane.

"I see it," said Don, "It's by the old oak tree that marks the cemetery boundary line."

"Yes, I see it. It's . . . it's a man. Who is he?" asked Jane.

The three stood shivering as the man walked in their direction.

"What's he wearing?" asked Jane.

"It looks like some kind of old seaman's outfit," answered Don.

The chill in the air deepened and the hair on the back of Don's neck prickled. A fog seemed to be rolling in behind the man even though it was a clear evening. The man stopped, then looked around as if searching for something.

The man walked over to a grave site and seemed to smile as if he had found whatever he was looking for. The fog rolled back from the man, then disappeared— and so did the man.

"I'm scared," moaned Barbara. "Let's get out of here."

"But wait," said Jane, "the fog is gone, and so is the chill."

"It's all right," said Don. "Come on, let's look at the headstone where the man disappeared."

It was warmer as the trio approached the grave site where the man had vanished into thin air. Don read the inscription on the headstone:

Jasper Whitehead
Born May 21, 1888
Lost at sea Dec. 2, 1912
We await your return.

"But . . . but . . ." both girls cried, "it's not possible! It can't be! But we did see him."

"Granny Putnum told me about this site," said Don. "There's no one buried here, just a memorial for the lost seaman. I think we just saw Jasper Whitehead come home to his final resting place."

MEMORIES

"HAVE YOU EVER HEARD OF SOMEONE traveling, like they have a double, only it's really that person but it's not a physical body?" asked Theresa, a busy woman in her thirties with three active children.

"My grandfather had died. As he got older he started closing himself off from the rest of the family. He seemed to start arguments with people just so he could cut them out of his life. He started one with my mother's family and we didn't see him, except when he was outside and we passed his house, for the last three years of his life.

"After he died, I spent a few nights in his house with Aunt Dale, my absolute favorite aunt. My grandfather's room was in the back of the house and that's where I slept. He had one of those old beds with the springs exposed. Every time I moved, the bed creaked. I knew I'd never get any sleep like that, so I got as comfortable as I could and tried not to move.

"I was finally just about to fall asleep when I suddenly jerked awake. I could hear the kitchen door opening. It couldn't have been Aunt Dale; she was at the opposite end of the house in her old bedroom. Besides, when she goes to bed, she falls right to sleep, out like a light.

"I could feel a cold sweat breaking out all over my skin, and I couldn't breathe as I tried to hear whoever was coming into the house. Then whoever it was started to walk across the kitchen floor."

Theresa grinned and laughed nervously. "You can bet I didn't turn my head and look when the footsteps stopped at my door. I pretended to be asleep, and eventually I did fall asleep. Being terrified wears you out.

"The next morning Aunt Dale asked me, first thing, if I'd been out the back door during the night. See, she found it standing wide open when she got up to make coffee the next morning."

"Sometime later that same year," Theresa continued, "I was asleep at home in my own room when something woke me up. I was instantly fully awake, and I could see Aunt Dale standing at the foot of my bed in front of my bureau, trying to turn on a lamp.

"I spoke to her but she didn't respond. She didn't even look at me. So I got out of bed and walked across the carpet to Aunt Dale. I spoke to her again, but she still didn't respond.

"I thought she was pulling some kind of joke, or maybe something bad had happened and she was thinking of a good way to tell me. Anyway, I reached out to touch her, and that's when she disappeared. Completely. She was gone and I was just left standing there.

"You'd think I would have been scared by something like that, but the strange thing is, I wasn't the least bit scared. I kind of shrugged it off and went back to bed, right back to sleep.

"Later, when I told my family, they thought I'd been dreaming. I hadn't been dreaming or sleepwalking. I've never walked in my sleep in my life. Aunt Dale was there in the room. I don't know why, she just was."

THE MAN IN
THE YELLOW SLICKER

BETH AND CHARLES BOWERS LOOKED forward to weekends when they would take their five-year-old daughter, Whitney, and escape the pollution of the city and go northward to the low-lying north Georgia mountains. They relished the fresh clean air and cold crisp rivers, the warm days and cool nights. And the people, so different, clinging to religion and family traditions handed down for generations. Every weekend was a wonderful adventure.

It was an old farm nestled against the Appalachian foothills that caught the attention of the Bowers family when they finally decided to break away and leave the rigors of city living. The place was almost like something from another time, a far distant past.

It was apparent that no one had lived on the farm for quite some time. Neglected for many years, it was in a sad, near-weeping state of disrepair. But the rambling two-story farmhouse with its wraparound porches had great potential. And the overlarge tin-roofed barn could serve as a double garage and workshop and still provide more storage room than they would ever need.

A pasture, now overgrown with brambles and tall spindly pine trees, had undoubtedly held cows at one time. The Bowers could envision show horses dancing and prancing there in the future, after they had done more than a bit of work to the barbed wire fences.

A new highway offered easy access to their city jobs, and being young and willing to make the efforts necessary to bring the old place up to date, they became obsessed with owning the farm.

Inquiries revealed the place was ten acres and available at more than a reasonable price. Beth wondered what history the place had but never bothered to ask anyone.

Six months later, renovations were well underway and the Bowers family moved in. All was wonderful in their rural world until one night when a terrible storm rumbled through the mountains. Lightning zigzagged across the night sky and torrential rains lashed against the windows in the howl of an angry wind. The electricity flickered, threatening to go off. After two hours of waiting for the storm's rage to pass, Beth and Charles decided it might be better to go to bed and try to sleep through the night and storm. Besides, they had no control over the weather, and waiting and worrying about possible danger wasn't changing anything.

It was agreed between the three of them that Whitney would sleep in her parents' room on a cot.

Whitney named all the doll babies she would need to bring from her room for the night as the threesome entered the stairway foyer.

Ready to step upon the landing, Beth's attention was drawn to a man descending the stairs. He appeared to be old and was wearing an aged yellow slicker. A rain hat was pulled far down on his head.

Charles grabbed Whitney in his arms and pulled Beth back into the living room. All the Bowerses were shocked at seeing the man in their house but made no sound; they just stared as the man continued his trek down the stairs and out the front door.

Hurrying to the window, they watched as the old man made his way across the yard into the barn. Coming to his senses somewhat, Charles ran out into the storm to follow and confront the intruder.

"He's gone," Charles exclaimed upon his return to the house. "I searched everywhere. He's not out there. He just disappeared."

The next day after the storm had passed and sunshine once more shone on their new home, the Bowerses sought answers to who the man could have been. They were told by an old-timer that it was probably Old Jake.

The story had been around so long it had been dismissed and forgotten long before. Jake had been the caretaker and handyman who had lived there sometime around the turn of the century with the Cochran family. The small attic had been his private room, and caring for the farm animals and machinery and handling other farm duties had been his job. He took his job very seriously, even sleeping in the barn with the animals when storms abounded in the night.

One night late in the springtime a big storm came up without warning. As Old Jake, dressed in his yellow slicker and hat, made his way to the barn to see about the animals, he suffered a heart attack and fell dead in the yard.

The Bowerses say they have seen Old Jake several times since that first night. It's always storming, and he's always wearing his yellow slicker and hat. He comes from the attic room, down the stairs, and makes his way to the barn.

By all accounts, Old Jake doesn't bother anything or anyone. He's just a man who still takes his duties seriously—even though his duties ended more than half a century ago.

THE DANCING SPRITE

"ABOUT THIRTY YEARS AGO," BEGAN
Louise Stamey, "my family and I were visiting my
mother's cousin. After supper we all went out on the
porch. It wasn't quite dark yet, but they had put on the
porch light. My mother and daddy and cousin Wilma and
her husband were chatting while my two younger sisters
and Wilma's children played in the yard."

Louise paused, seeming puzzled as she remembered
the strange incident that had happened so long ago.

"I walked across the yard and down by the road. I
was just moseying along when I heard, well, a giggle, I
guess. I looked across the road at an old house that
Cousin Wilma said had been empty for years. Supposedly some kind of tragedy had happened there.

"Then I saw something—or someone—jumping
around, like it was playing leapfrog on a fire hydrant. But
there was no fire hydrant there since this was thirty years
ago in the North Carolina mountains.

"I got a good look at it from the side. It was a person.
It looked like a young child about seven or eight years old.
Then it turned toward me, and I gasped in horror. This
person or child or whatever it was had no facial features

at all. No eyes, no nose, no lips, and no mouth—just a blank face. Yet I had heard it giggle.

"What made it stranger still was that my sisters and the grown-ups were not more than forty feet away from where I stood, and yet none had seen the faceless child but me.

"Anyway, we left the next morning. I was sitting in the back seat of the car with my sisters, and when I looked out the rear window, there it was, dancing and leaping in the middle of the road. The morning was bright and sunny, and I could see that it still had a blank face, completely devoid of any features. I'll never forget it."

THE RETURN

For FIFTY YEARS OR MORE THE OLD MEN of Carpenter County met in the little mountain town of Paramour, the county seat. The town itself was little more than a wide place in the road, but it boasted a barber shop, drugstore, dry goods, pool hall, five-and-dime, and a hardware store. It was in front of the hardware store that the old men gathered, sitting in weathered straight-backed chairs, when Saturdays brought them to town. They kept up with all the goings-on in the county, from politics to religion, as the Saturdays piled one on top of another. As the years passed, one by one all the old men died.

The old store changed hands many times, as did the merchandise it sold. Over time the old straight-backed chairs were removed and replaced with lawn mowers, bicycles, racks of hanging dresses, or nothing at all.

The most recent business to occupy the building is a furniture store, and once more chairs grace the sidewalk out front. Some are rocking chairs and others are fashioned in the styles of chairs that had sat there many years before. But these chairs are there to attract customers. They are all shiny and new, and people are discouraged from sitting in them.

The Return

It has been reported by some of the old-timers that on Saturdays passersby occasionally can see the chairs rocking. They rock in the gentle breezes that float among the foothills, and at times they rock when the air is completely still. Sometimes faint, gravelly voices and laughter can be heard, as if the old men were still there, telling yarns as they did years ago.

Is it possible that over time the old men have returned to their once accustomed places to resume their Saturday visits in the rural reaches of Appalachia, where word of mouth is still the best way to keep up with all the goings-on, from politics to religion?

HANGMAN'S ROPE

"BACK THEN THEY HAD ROPE BEDS," SAID
Bertha as she began to relate an eerie tale that happened
to her family. "Grandpa wasn't feeling too good, so
Grandma said for him to stay in bed. Grandpa said he
would like the corn-shuck mattress taken off since he
thought he might feel better just lying on the ropes.

"Grandma went outside to get eggs and check the
garden. She got the eggs, pulled up some weeds, and
picked three tomatoes, then she came back into the house
through the kitchen and walked toward the bedroom
where Grandpa was.

"The front door of their house would not stay shut.
They would slam it shut and turn away, and that darn
door would fly open.

"Well, as Grandma was walking toward the bedroom, the front door burst open. She ran to it and looked
out, but no one was there.

"Grandma went back to the bedroom, and there
was Grandpa with blood all over his face. It looked
like someone had tried to stomp him through the
rope bed. Grandma yelled for Uncle William and then
asked Grandpa what had happened. Who had done this
to him?

" 'I don't know,' said Grandpa. 'I didn't see anybody, and no one hit me. I thought I was in a earthquake. The rope bed just kept jumping around, but I couldn't get out of it.'

"Grandpa got better," continued Bertha. "But a funny thing happened. Grandma fixed the rope bed, but after Grandpa's experience no one could ever sleep in it again. It would jerk and jump around so that one would have to get out of it. Grandma even put the bed in another room, but when somebody tried to lay down in it, it would toss them out onto the floor.

"Cousin Harlon was a deputy sheriff, and he and his wife, being a young couple, vowed to spend the night in the weird bed.

"Grandma said it couldn't have been more than ten minutes after Harlon and his wife had gone off to bed that they came tearing out of the bedroom, pale as ghosts. And just before they got to the front door, it burst open. It was almost as if someone, or something, was running in front of them."

Bertha smiled and added, "Grandma found out later that the rope used to make the bed was once the county hangman's rope."

THE COLD, COLD HAND

THE MOUNTAINS IN AND AROUND SOUTHERN
Appalachia have always had their rebellious youth.
Maybe it's boredom or not having any city-life excitement. Or maybe it's just plain meanness in some. But in
years past it was believed that, as a general rule, a bad
boy turned into a bad man. So folks noticed how
young'uns acted, and formed their opinions, and waited
to see if they held true. Few missed the mark by far. But
David Miller proved to be an exception.

When David was about twenty-three years old, he
was a hell-raiser, to say the least. He drove his old car in
a reckless fashion and drank till he was passed out cold
near every night. He dared life to defy his way of living
on a daily basis. David couldn't, or wouldn't, hold a job
for any length of time because of his bad temper and his
"don't care" attitude.

The older folks in Washington County said that
David was "the devil's own."

But when the young man tried, he could charm the
birds right out of the trees. And the young girls didn't
really stand a chance against his sparkling coal-black
eyes and lopsided grin. His hair, curly and dark, appeared to frame the olive-skinned face of an angel when

he turned his charms to attract the innocent girls waiting for his attentions.

Many was the night David would drag himself home near dawn, drunk and bloody from some beer-joint brawl. His parents would clean him up and put him to bed to sleep it off and allow his body a few hours to begin the healing process. Sometimes he'd be so battered his father would have to take him down the mountain to Dr. Simmons's house for stitches or to set dislocated or broken bones.

"You're never going to see twenty-five, son," said the doctor one night as he put a cast on David's broken hand, "if you don't change your ways and stop running with the devil."

The young man laughed as his father added, "It's really a shame, David, and it hurts me and your mama so bad to see you wasting your life. You're going to hell, son, and even all your mama's praying ain't gonna help none if you don't help yourself."

"Ain't got there yet," groaned the young man as he winced in pain from several broken ribs. "Maybe tomorrow."

By the time David and his father arrived home, dawn was cracking the eastern sky above the Appalachian foothills. David went straight to bed, and the last thing he heard was his mama praying, asking the Almighty to look after her son because she couldn't.

David was a changed man after that night. He stopped fighting and drinking and staying out all night. He even got a job at the sawmill and proved to be a good worker.

Parents still warned their young daughters to keep away from David Miller, but the girls were still drawn to his dangerous reputation and good looks.

After some months, David appeared to have settled down completely. He began courting a young woman named Hanna Bishop, who lived just across the county line, and in the fall, they married and moved into a small house on her parents' farm. David kept his job at the sawmill and tried hard to live down his reckless past, even joining the church and being baptized.

Years passed and two boys were born to David and Hanna. They made good parents to the boys, who both had dark curly hair, coal-black eyes, olive skin, and lopsided grins.

When Ernest, the older boy, fell off the barn and broke his arm one Saturday in early spring, David got him into the car and drove like a madman to Dr. Simmons's house.

The doctor set the bone easily enough and put a cast on Ernest's arm, then gave the boy an injection of antibiotics and a tetanus shot. The doctor's wife, Milly, who was also a nurse, gave Ernest something for his pain and a mild sedative to calm him.

"Let's let him rest for half an hour or so to see if the pain's going to stop or if he's going to have any kind of reaction to the medicine. Milly will stay with him," said old Dr. Simmons, nodding toward his wife. "We'll have some coffee in the kitchen while we wait." Turning his attention to David, he added, "He'll do better if you're not hovering."

David assured his son that he'd be in the next room, then followed the old man to the kitchen. He sat down at the kitchen table while Dr. Simmons poured coffee from the enamel pot sitting on the back of the wood-burning stove.

"Still hot," said the doctor, sitting down across from David and sliding one of the two cups across the table to the young man.

David accepted the coffee gratefully. He took a sip of the hot brew, then ran a hand wearily through his dark curly hair. He gave out a long sigh and shook his head.

"You sure my boy's going to be okay, Doc?" David asked.

"You always were," the old man answered. "But I got to tell you, sometimes I had my doubts whether you'd live through another episode or not. What made you change? What was it that turned you around?"

David drew in a deep breath and let it out slowly, then looked at the doctor who had patched him up too many times to count and said, "I got away."

"From what?" asked Dr. Simmons.

"I ain't never told nobody," said David slowly, "because I figured nobody'd ever believe me in a million years. Well, maybe Mama, but she never asked me. But you know how Mama is. She probably knew anyway."

"I've always known you to be truthful, David," the old doctor said, now more curious than ever to hear the story and hoping to encourage David to talk.

"Well, it was right after I got in that fight over at Bud's Bar and you fixed up my broke hand and busted ribs. I really took a beating that time."

The young man flexed his fingers, turning his hand back and forth as if checking its mobility, then continued.

"After me and Daddy left here that night, we drove home. Daddy didn't talk, and my head hurt so bad I couldn't if I wanted to. Best I can recall, Daddy got me into bed about daylight, and I think Mama was praying when I went to sleep.

"I don't know how long I slept, but when I woke up, it was dark as night and storming so bad the whole house was shaking. I kinda got my senses back and figured out where I was. Then I discovered I couldn't move my hand and arm. Not the hand I broke, the other one. It was hanging down off the bed."

David stopped and took another sip of coffee. He continued to look at his hand, which was trembling. Clenching it into a fist, he continued.

"In what seemed like an instant, I was stone cold and wet with sweat. My heart was pounding so hard I thought it would burst, and I couldn't draw a breath. I knew I was dying, and the devil had me by the hand. He was pulling me, and that's why I couldn't move my arm. I can't really tell you in words; maybe there ain't none. You just can't know how scared I was with death on me and the devil pulling me into hell.

"Hearing Mama praying clicked somewhere inside me and I thought, 'God, help me!' As soon as I thought that, lightning cracked and my room lit up blue-white, and I knew if I didn't loose myself right then I never would. I'd never have another chance.

" 'God help me, please!' I thought again and pulled hard. In that split second I was loosed. The devil let go of me and I was free! The storm seemed to stop. I drew a long breath. My lungs burned awful, it had been so long since they'd had any air. I promised right then that I'd stop my reckless ways. And I've tried.

"I believe if the storm hadn't woke me and the good Lord hadn't heard my silent prayer, I'd be in hell right now," said David as if swearing an oath.

The kitchen became quiet. There was nothing more to tell of David Miller's story. The old doctor nodded and cleared his throat as Mrs. Simmons stepped into the room.

"Ernest is ready to go home, now. He's going to be just fine," she said with a smile.

"That's good to hear," said David. He rose from the chair, then got his boy and went home to his wife and younger son who waited anxiously for their return.

RESIDENT GHOST

KRIS KELLY WAS A CHILD OF DIVORCED
parents. She lived with her mother and brother in a modest house in a small town in the mountains of North Carolina. Shortly after the divorce, her father moved to another town and, with the passing of time, remarried and bought a house.

The house was only about fifteen years old. Not exactly newly built, but not old by any means. Its colonial split-level style and backyard pool set it apart as being particularly grand in the low-lying foothills.

Kris was nine years old when she made her first visit. Tom, her father, and Mary, her stepmother, casually joked about the resident ghost living in their house. Kris didn't realize it wasn't something to laugh about but was real in every sense of the word.

Night had fallen when they arrived, and as bedtime came, Tom was called in to work. He was a fireman and always on call.

Kris couldn't explain the eeriness surrounding her, yet she knew the house had a presence, almost as if it were a being unto itself. She did not want to be alone upstairs with her father gone, so she asked to sleep downstairs with Mary.

Sometime late that night, for no apparent reason, Kris suddenly awakened. She was startled by her surroundings, and it took a few seconds to remember where she was. Then her vision was drawn across the bedroom, through the open door to the den. A lamp had been left on and its soft light illuminated the darkness.

Kris's heart jumped, then raced when she saw something floating in front of the fireplace. It had human form and a milky transparency to it. It didn't move or make any sound at all. Kris quickly woke her stepmother.

"Look! There's something in the den," she whispered in cold fear.

Mary roused herself, retrieved her glasses from the bedside table, and looked in the direction Kris indicated.

"Do you see it? What is it?" The little girl asked in a quivering voice.

"It won't hurt you. Go back to sleep," came the reply from Mary as they both stared at whatever was in front of the fireplace in the adjoining room.

As soon as the words were spoken, the wispy apparition faded away.

Kris was afraid to go back to sleep and nervously kept asking questions, trying to keep her stepmother awake.

"What was that? Didn't that scare you? Have you seen it before?" she asked, scooting her small frame closer to Mary.

"We see it all the time," Mary said. "Go back to sleep. It's nothing."

Kris finally slept and in the morning woke to find herself in the upstairs bed. Her father had returned during the night and moved her. Kris saw nothing else during that visit, yet she knew that something, perhaps the house itself, was watching her.

She made several visits over time, but that strange, uneasy feeling that came over her was the only evidence that the house held something—something that couldn't be explained.

When Kris was thirteen, she went to spend her summer vacation with Tom and Mary. With a score of books, suntanning lotion, and two swimsuits, she planned to take advantage of their backyard pool and the warm summer sun. Kris wasn't really afraid of the house and agreed to stay there alone while Tom and Mary worked. After all, they had a telephone and Kris could call if any trouble arose.

Even though much of the mountain areas had prospered somewhat over time and new houses and weekend cabins dotted the landscape, the Kellys' home was still secluded, with the nearest neighbor a mile or more away. Kris never thought of the isolation as being bad, but as privacy to lounge around in her bikini without worrying about the prying eyes of strangers.

It was a warm Tuesday morning as Kris donned her bikini and went out to swim and soak up the sun's rays. After a couple of hours, hunger as well as her daily soap operas pulled at her. A shower, lunch, and her television stories would fill the afternoon, and then she would begin supper.

Kris was hurrying to get a change of clothes from her bureau when she first heard a strange bumping sound in the bathroom adjoining the bedroom. She dismissed it as wind blowing through the window or just general house grumbles and continued searching the bureau drawers.

The noise grew louder and more rhythmic. Kris turned and saw the window was closed. She also saw the vanity cabinet doors rapidly opening and banging shut, and they were doing it all on their own. No one was pushing or pulling on them to cause the movements. Kris was frozen with fear as she watched and heard the bathroom come to angry life in front of her. The action became louder and louder and faster and faster—and so did Kris's fear.

"Move!" she told herself. "Get out!"

Kris was paralyzed. Her heart raced one beat over another, her head pounded, and she couldn't breathe.

"Get out! Get out!" she shouted in her mind.

In an instant, like crystal shattering, Kris broke free from her trancelike state and ran. She ran from the angry spirits; she ran from the evil warning her to leave; she ran from the house itself.

Tom found Kris huddled against the fence at the far end of the pool when he and Mary came home from work. Kris was hysterical as the experience played over and over in her mind.

Kris refused to go back inside the house, so Tom took her to stay with an aunt living several miles away. The young teen recovered quickly from her ordeal, but she has never forgotten the experience. Nor has she ever again set foot inside her father's house with its resident ghost.

FOOTSTEPS IN THE NIGHT

KRIS KELLY'S BROTHER, BUD, HAD NEVER spent a night in their father and stepmother's house. So it wasn't surprising that Bud had laughed at Kris's tales of an evil presence in the home.

"Shucks, Kris," said Bud, "that house is only fifteen years old. It can't have a ghost in it. Besides, nothing ever happened there."

Just before Bud was to go away to college he accepted an invitation to spend his last night with his father and stepmother. They had an enjoyable evening, and at 11:00 P.M. everyone decided to go to bed. Bud headed to his bedroom, which was over the kitchen.

Now Bud was a typical teenager and had made arrangements with his friends to go out one more night with them. So with shoes in hand, he tiptoed down the staircase. He laughed to himself as he thought of his sister Kris. "I haven't seen anything of her so-called ghost," he thought.

Bud reached the first floor and carefully tiptoed across the hardwood floor to the kitchen. He stood by the window on the left side of the kitchen so he could watch the road for his friends who were coming to pick him up.

It was strangely still in the house. Even the usual house noises seemed to have disappeared.

"What was that?" Bud said aloud as something that sounded like faint footsteps echoed in the night.

He heard it again. Someone was pacing in the room above him, his bedroom.

The pacing increased in volume and Bud thought, "Oh, boy, it's Dad, and he's going to catch me sneaking out."

The footsteps in the bedroom stopped, then Bud heard them going down the hall.

"Uh-oh, I'm in the soup," he said under his breath. The footsteps got louder as they came down the stairs, then completely stopped when they reached the bottom. After a moment, heavy footsteps came down the hall toward the kitchen.

Bud stood silently against the wall by the kitchen door. "Maybe it's Kris's evil spirit," he muttered to himself, then dismissed the thought. "No, it's Dad, and I'm in trouble."

The footsteps reached the kitchen door and stopped. Bud waited but no one came through the door. He didn't know if it was his imagination, but he could hear heavy breathing.

Finally, Bud looked around the corner and saw—no one. Nobody was there. Bud raced down the hall and up the stairs to his father's bedroom, but when he looked in, both his father and stepmother were sound asleep.

Bud never laughed at Kris's tales of an evil presence again, for he knew deep in his heart that those footsteps were from an evil haunt. The next day Bud left for college, and the sun never set with him in that house where an evil force resided.

PANTHER

GRANNY STONE CLAIMED SHE COULD remember clear back to the day she was born. Sometimes she would say she remembered what it was like before she was born. She could also remember a thousand and one ghost stories and was always a little proud when one of her granddaughters or one of their friends asked her to tell a story.

Summer or winter, they would gather in the bedroom Granny shared with her five granddaughters—minus two, now that the eldest ones were married and living in homes of their own. Granny would look at their expectant young faces and grant their request, her voice quavering a bit with age, which only added to the appeal of her storytelling.

With her blue-veined hands folded atop her apron and the lenses of her round, gold-rimmed eyeglasses shining in the light of the naked bulb overhead, Granny would begin:

"This was before you was born, before I was born even. This was about the time when my mommy married my daddy. About the time folks around here began to talk of a panther killing chickens and dogs and such.

"One morning a feller turned up missing. At first

everybody thought he had run off from his wife. There was seven children in the family, and he was rather more fond of moonshine than necessary. But then his horse showed up, all shaking and nervous, and on its hind parts was two long, gouged, bloody places that looked like a large, clawed animal had raked the horse."

Granny made her bony, long, tough-nailed hands into claws, and her eyes blazed fiercely behind the lenses of her glasses. The girls huddled together on the patch-work quilts covering the iron bed, held their collective breath, and looked one at the other.

"The man was never found alive, and the horse weren't fit for no kind of work after that. Couldn't plow nor pull a wagon, and so that widow woman was left by herself without a good horse to help her with the work on the farm and no way to buy another, for a man overfond of drink don't leave much money nor good credit behind when he goes."

Granny pursed her lips, obviously thinking less of the man than of the panther that probably got him.

"After a little bit, the men got together after meeting one Sunday and decided they would hunt this panther down for they feared it would get another man along with all the chickens and dogs and even hogs. So they started looking for fresh signs of it. They'd go during the day when they got the spare time, for panthers hunted at night and laid up during the day.

"Finally, they found it in its den, and it being day, there weren't hardly any trouble shooting it. From snout to twitching tail that creature was fully twelve feet long and had a coat as black as the night. A beautiful thing it was, but deadly. In its den the hunter men found not one but two human skeletons, picked clean and scattered along with chickens and dogs and hogs and deer. Everybody figured one body was the drunkard, but it never come to them who else had died of the panther, though the county policeman checked around. But that ain't the end of the story.

"When I was a girl, fully twenty years after that panther was killed in its den and the two sets of human bones put into the ground with proper burials, a man told of being chased by a black panther late one night when the moon cast her shadow on the ground almost as bright as the sun.

"The man was coming home from a dance and singing. He had his fiddle strapped to his saddle and was just taking his time going home 'cause it was such a pleasant spring night. About the time he had most fallen asleep on horseback, he heard a scream so like a woman's that he thought one was being killed in the woods either side of the road. He thought to help this woman who was in mortal danger when he heard a thrashing in the woods and out jumped an animal of such size and blackness, he thought it was a bear."

The little, narrow-shouldered woman made herself as big as she could, spreading her skinny arms and looking at the girls with a stern stare.

"But it wasn't a bear. It was a panther. A rare sight in those days for they'd been hunted down and mostly killed by then. But that wasn't what the man was thinking. His only thought was on getting out of there. His horse had the same thought and decided to put as much distance between them and the panther as it could. It set off through the woods and right behind it came the panther, screaming every little bit just to scare the sin out of man and the skin off a horse.

"Off they run for what seemed like hours. Up hill and down into gully, through last year's blackberries and around a thicket of mountain laurel. All the while that panther was right with them, never losing a step.

"Finally, the horse went off into Scarecorn Creek, fortunate for man and horse that it was the shallows and not a rocky spot. The man looked back to see if the panther would follow, and what do you suppose he saw?"

The girls shook their heads. They were too caught up in the story to have a thought in their minds.

Granny leaned forward and lowered her voice. "He saw that black panther gather itself up for the jump across that creek and he saw it push off the bank. Oh, I'm sure it was a sight to behold, there in the moonlight.

"And then he saw it . . ." she paused for effect, ". . . disappear, quick as a wink. One minute it was there, the next it wasn't."

Granny eased back in her armchair, and one side of her mouth pulled up into an almost smile. "Now what do you think of that?"

As the girls shook their heads and clung to each other, Granny supposed they would think twice about going to the outhouse from now on, even during the day.

PREMONITIONS

THE BLUE RIDGE MOUNTAINS OF THE Appalachian foothill chain in Georgia, Tennessee, and North Carolina hold secrets as old as time. Some of the inhabitants of these mountains hold secrets, too. Some have talents to see into the future. Others have a "knowing" somewhere inside themselves that tells what their own future holds, and they understand beyond any shadow of doubt that this thing, this knowing, is simply fate and that nothing can change it in life or in death.

Sabra Haggen had this knowing, and when she and her two sisters were helping with the laying out of their dead mother, she told them about her own funeral. She even spoke of how and when she would die.

The sisters tried to hush her, saying her talk was just the ramblings of someone heavy with grief over losing a loved one. They also said her talk was morbid and if others heard her, she might be considered crazy or possessed. But Sabra continued with details until she had voiced every last one.

One sister, Becky, became angry and said Sabra was being just plain mean and thoughtless and wanted attention and should be ashamed for acting up so in front of the preacher's wife and a cousin, who were also helping with the body.

Catherine, the other sister, became so overwhelmed that someone else close to her would die and leave her that she had to leave the room in a crying fit of nerves. Sabra's words weren't spoken sadly, just matter-of-factly.

When Sabra had finished telling how things would be, she smiled sincerely and said, "Just wait and see. See if what I say ain't so."

Nobody said anything to Sabra, not wanting to encourage her to say anything more. And so it was quiet after that and the task of laying out the old mother was finished in silence.

For several weeks following the funeral, Catherine and Becky, along with the cousin, stayed away from Sabra as much as possible, afraid that she'd "set in" again. Of course, the preacher's wife couldn't ignore Sabra as it was one of her duties to minister to the bereaved and console them in their time of mourning. But to the best of everyone's knowledge, Sabra's death and funeral weren't mentioned by any of the women ever again.

Years passed and all the sisters married and had children, who in turn grew up and had families of their own. Life had indeed been kind to this mountain family. They had remained close enough geographically to visit and close enough in family ties to want to.

Sabra, at age fifty-three, was the first of the sisters to die. After the funeral, the family gathered at Catherine's house to reminisce, mourn, and begin the healing process without one of their own.

While sitting in the living room remembering and talking about childhood, the cousin, Mary Ellen, recalled when Sabra's mother died and the remarks Sabra had made about her own death.

"Well, she said she'd die at age fifty-three of a

stroke," Mary Ellen said. "And she did. Isn't it strange how I would think of that?"

Becky looked about her and broke into sobs. "And she said I'd wear green and Catherine blue and even her own dress would be yellow. How did she know?" she cried.

"And," said the cousin, adding to the remembrance, "the songs. They were right."

"And so was her flowers," said Becky.

"A blanket of red carnations and a wreath of white aster mums at the head of her casket and yellow and bronze ones at the foot," Catherine said softly. "I remembered her words today as Preacher Barrell was talking over her and saw it all. Everything was just like she said it would be. I even asked her daughter, Clara, after the service, who had made the arrangements. She said they just left everything up to the funeral home, seeing as how they was just too upset and shocked by her sudden death."

Wiping the tears from her eyes with a handkerchief, Catherine continued, "Clara asked if I thought her mother would have liked the way things were done, and I just told her it was very nice and I felt sure Sabra would have smiled with approval."

LETTING GO

THE WOMAN WAS OLD, NINETY-FOUR TO be exact. Her body was worn out and she was sick of living. She was confined to a nursing home, and even though her children and their families visited daily, she longed for Arthur, her husband, now dead for twenty-odd years.

Southern Appalachia had changed from the time the woman's mother was old and she had looked after her mother's needs. Life was made easier by professional nursing care now, and people were encouraged to live by good nutrition and medication. Some were even forced to live by machines, rather than letting nature have its way.

The old woman's daughter, Ellen, though she worked every day, made time to visit her mother regularly and tried to comfort her in her declining years. They talked of younger years and better times. The old woman liked to remember life as it was then on the farm with her children and her beloved Arthur, tending the fields and livestock.

As time passed, Ellen saw the misery in her mother's eyes and decided that maybe she, in her desire to keep her mother close, was somehow responsible for her mother's pain and suffering.

Ellen sat at the bedside for a long time watching her mother sleep one day. When the old woman awoke, she faced her daughter with a weary smile. The old woman knew Ellen would be there, as she always was, when she woke from her morning nap. Ellen had always been dedicated and devoted to her parents. Even as a child she had been loving and conscious of her parents and the sacrifices they made for her.

"Are you happy, Mother?" asked Ellen very softly.

"No, child," came the answer in a bare whisper.

"Do you want to go? Do you want to go be with Papa?" Ellen asked in a shaky voice.

Tears trickled from the corners of her old mother's eyes.

Ellen drew a deep breath and gently took her mother's aged, wrinkled hands in hers. "You don't have to stay here, Mother," she said tenderly. "You can go on. You've lived a long life and your family can make it. We'll miss you, but we can make it."

The old woman looked at Ellen with a puzzled look on her face but said nothing.

"The angels will come and get you and take you to heaven to be with Papa," Ellen continued lovingly.

A peaceful look came to the old woman's face as she looked more closely at her daughter. "I can go?" she asked.

"Yes, Mother. You can go. I love you," Ellen said, reaching to place a kiss on the aged, wrinkled brow of the woman before her.

The little woman loosed her hands from her daughter's and lifted both arms high, toward heaven. Ellen sat reverently as her mother reached for something beyond Ellen's view. Within three hours the old woman had died. She passed silently, serenely, and at peace, knowing at long last that it was time.

REMINDERS

PEOPLE IN THE SOUTHERN MOUNTAINS hardly ever saw a doctor for their medical needs in times past. Occasionally, one was needed for setting severely broken bones or stitching deep wounds, but folks generally did their own doctoring.

Pregnancy and birthing were as natural as breathing, and were, after all, important parts of following God's Word to replenish the earth. It was believed He would take care of His own. However, midwives, or "granny women," were sometimes called upon to help bring babies into the world, slap their bottoms to draw the first breath of life into their lungs, and inform the fathers of the newest addition to the family.

Seventeen-year-old Dorie Grafton and Isaac, her young husband of almost a year, anxiously awaited their first child. Isaac's grandmother was a midwife and was anxious to help bring the first of this new generation into the world.

Dorie was sick a lot in the beginning, but after several weeks of birch bark and cornbread-crust tea at the onset of morning sickness, it gradually subsided. She was young and strong, and besides, she was only pregnant, not ailing from any life-threatening disorder.

Four months into the pregnancy, Dorie was showing a nice round belly and was no longer able to fit into her dresses. She made do with a couple of Isaac's old shirts and a cast-off dress Granny Grafton brought her.

"I specs you might be carrying two babies from your size," said Granny Grafton on the day she brought the dress.

Dorie was pleased and Isaac was beside himself with joy. The little two-room cabin would need some adding-on in a few years, she mused, if they kept on bringing babies two at a time.

Six months into the pregnancy, Dorie was huge. Her feet swelled and her face was puffy, and her back never stopped hurting.

"This is just how it is with some," said Granny Grafton. "Nothing to worry yourself about."

Daily chores became almost impossible by the end of the seventh month, and Dorie realized this was not normal. She'd been around enough pregnant women in her family to know that she was too big. The never-ending back pain was almost unbearable at times, but the kicks and turns of the baby or babies inside her helped Dorie endure.

Isaac rubbed her back and drew cool water from the well to soak her tired and aching feet at the end of his long day's work in the field. He hoped to have the stumps pulled and the ground turned before his child was born.

"Won't be long," said Isaac one night as he rubbed Dorie's back with callused hands. "I'm gonna start on the cradle soon as I get the wood planed. I cut it weeks ago. Ought to be seasoned by now."

Dorie smiled, both at his words and at his strong hands rubbing the weariness from her back. She turned to face him. The baby was kicking, and Dorie placed his hand on her stomach.

Isaac's eyes grew wide as he felt the hard thrusts and saw the little bulges appear here and there through the tightly stretched material of Dorie's old dress.

"Must be some kind of ruckus going on in there," he said.

"Always is," she answered, wondering if it would ever stop.

Two days later, it did. All movement stopped, and the stillness inside Dorie was worse than a storm. Granny Grafton came to check on her and confirmed her fears: the baby was dead.

Dorie cried and Isaac seemed to grow old overnight, worrying over what sin they were being punished for. Dorie kept carrying the child inside her, even though there was no life. She was told, "Nature will take care of it."

After three weeks of waiting for nature to take over, Granny Grafton came and gave Dorie an herb potion that threw her into extreme hard labor. After sixteen hours, she delivered a stillborn son.

Granny Grafton and Isaac buried the baby under a huge hickory tree on the hillside beyond the barn, and marked the grave with a tiny wooden cross.

Time passed and both Dorie and Isaac recovered from the ordeal, but they never had any other children.

Dorie said years later that she could still feel a baby's kicks in her belly and could occasionally hear, from somewhere deep inside her, the cry of an unborn child.

GRACE

SHE WAS ALWAYS AMAZED WHEN SHE looked at the little girl and realized that the child, golden as sunlight, was her own. There had been such a long wait for Megan. When Carolyn was thirty-two, Megan decided to be born.

And now Megan was four, talking all the time and able to stay within the lines when coloring. Carolyn and Tom, her husband, sometimes just sat and watched Megan, their first and only child, and wondered what she would be when she grew up.

Each time Megan was sick, the couple would be in near panic, fearing that something serious would happen and they would lose their precious baby. She suffered the usual childhood ailments, fevers and colic and such, but she always got better. Fortunately, there was someone else looking out for Megan besides Carolyn and Tom.

Once, in the middle of the night, Megan's temperature went up to 103 degrees. Carolyn knew that the child's body temperature should fall when she slept at night, but Megan's seemed to be going up. A trip to the emergency room was the only solution for the frightened parents, so Tom pulled on his coat and went to warm up the car.

Feeling torn between getting ready to go to the emergency room and staying and watching over her child, Carolyn heard Tom opening and closing the kitchen door and crossing the floor. She called to him that she was going to get dressed and put a few things into a bag in case she had to stay at the hospital. She would just be a minute if he would watch over Megan.

Carolyn hurriedly pulled on the clothes she'd worn the day before, gathered up what she thought she might need for a stay in the hospital and stuffed it into her already heavy pocketbook, then rushed back to the baby's room, her tennis shoes under one arm and the pocketbook under the other. When she entered the cheerful little room with the storybook wallpaper, Carolyn dropped both the shoes and the pocketbook in utter surprise.

An elderly woman wearing a purple print dress of summer-weight cotton turned her head only slightly at the noise. She was leaning over the Jenny Lind crib, gently stroking Megan's flushed cheek. When Carolyn approached her, the elderly woman simply disappeared.

Rather than frightening Carolyn, the appearance of the old woman calmed her. For the remainder of the ordeal she kept a cool head, but Tom was at a loss. Carolyn had been running about in near panic, then her demeanor changed drastically. It made no sense to Tom, not even after Carolyn told him what she had seen.

"But you don't understand," she said with a shake of her head. "It was Aunt Grace, Granny's sister. She always came when people were sick. It was like she knew exactly what to do. When I saw Aunt Grace, I realized everything would be all right."

The next time Megan was sick, Aunt Grace came again—and she came every time after that, although Carolyn could not always see her. Sometimes there was just a feeling of calm and reason that descended.

And now Megan was four, and Carolyn was watching her only child, playing with an older cousin, without a care in the world except trying to figure out how hard-cased snapdragons could suddenly burst to life in the closed palm of her small hands.

Carolyn and her sister Donna were sitting on the front porch of Donna's house. The sisters lived less than a hundred feet apart, but now they were much closer than when they actually shared a room. They often sat at the end of the day, talking about this and that, but today a very important subject had come to light.

"You've seen her too?" Carolyn asked, and she felt her heart lifting. "I thought no one else could see her. Tom doesn't, or he refuses to admit that he does. But I've seen her, usually when I've left the room for a minute and Megan is alone. I'll walk back into the room and there she'll be."

"Otherwise," Donna said, "you just know she's there with you, just like when we were little."

The sisters looked at their daughters as the girls explored the tree-shaded yard together. "I wonder if they know," Carolyn said. "Sometimes I'll hear Megan chattering away and I'll ask her who she was talking to, and she'll say it was to her secret friend, but she won't say anything else."

"Kendra's seen her," Donna said. "She told me the old woman looked like Grandma's sister. We have Aunt Grace's picture on the piano."

Suddenly, Carolyn smiled just a little. "Do you suppose Aunt Grace visits anyone else when they're sick?"

"I don't know," Donna said, a faraway look in her eyes. "I wouldn't want to get her into any kind of trouble. There might be hard feelings if it turns out she only visits us."

Both women laughed, knowing that family loyalties were deeply ingrained and that love and concern could survive, even after death.

SPRING PLACE

STRANGE HAPPENINGS ARE FRQUENTLY associated with water. For reasons unknown to the long-time inhabitants of the Appalachian foothills, many have heard about or experienced hauntings where water once was or still runs icy cold and clear. It holds reflections of time and reveals, to some, stories of the past that perhaps have been forgotten with time's passage.

James Smith, a young family man living on the old homeplace of his wife, asked his father-in-law, William, about the old spring place alongside the road between their houses.

William was stunned by the question and inquired further about what the young man meant.

"I get a funny feeling," James said, "every time I pass the spring place there in the dip of the road. It's like somebody or something is watching me. I've looked to see if anybody's there, but there never is. A few times I've had the hair on the back of my neck stand straight out.

"I've run a few times to get past there when it's dusky dark, but when I'm past the dip and nearly into the yard, the feeling goes away and I feel silly that I was scared. Well, maybe not scared, but uneasy. I don't know how to explain it. There's just something there and I wondered if you'd ever noticed it."

"No," William answered. "I ain't ever felt nothing."

William forgot the conversation as time passed, until one day when his youngest son, who was on his way out to play, said, "I don't like to go by the spring. When I ride my bicycle there on the road, I want to go fast as I can."

"Why?" asked Mary Ruth, his mother, as William stood by silently, recalling the conversation between James and himself maybe a year or so ago.

"I always feel like somebody is hiding somewhere and watching me," the youngster said. "When I get on by there, I always look all around and in the woods, but I don't see nobody. I don't feel like that anywhere else, just at the spring place."

"Don't be afraid," said Mary Ruth. "Mama and Daddy are always close by when you play outside."

The little boy nodded and sauntered outside to enjoy the warm day ahead of him while William and Mary Ruth readied themselves for a day in the chicken houses. They had three commercial chicken houses that produced hundreds of eggs each day, and collecting them and readying them for pick-up made for a very long day. But above all else, the business allowed them to stay at home with their children, and they would now listen more closely for cries of distress when the youngsters played around the spring place.

As the business grew, William hired Lucy Miller, a neighbor, to help in the chicken houses. She lived in a trailer on top of the rise on the other side of the spring.

Mary Ruth liked Lucy and found it nice to have someone to talk to while grading and sorting the eggs. One day, the spring place came up in their conversation.

"You know, that place kinda spooks me," Lucy said.

"Why?" asked Mary Ruth, busy placing eggs in large cardboard crates.

"It's always been spooky to me," Lucy said. "But one night during the summertime, I was sitting outside and I felt like somebody was watching me—you know, staring. I looked around but didn't see a soul anywhere. But that feeling was so strong I went inside and locked the doors. I turned on the television and still had that feeling. I finally closed the curtains."

"I've never felt anything like that," said Mary Ruth, "but my little boy has and James has, too."

"I like being outside," said Lucy. "But when it gets dusky dark, I go inside and lock up the doors and pull the curtains, 'cause I still get that feeling that there is somebody watching me. And the feeling comes from the old spring place."

Time and seasons passed, and the spring place wasn't mentioned again until years later when William's aunt came to visit.

"I'd like to go down to the old spring," the old woman said. "Always a spooky place when I was a girl. I would try to imagine how forlorn that young woman must have been to have hung herself down there when she heard her man had been killed in the Civil War."

MULE MOUNTAIN

STRANGE NAMES WERE OFTEN GIVEN TO the hills, hollers, creeks, and mountains in the Appalachian foothills. They were landmarks to the folks living in and around the area in times past. Mule Mountain was such a place.

"There. Up there," Richard Waters said. "I squirrel-hunted all these hollers and tops when I was a kid. Your daddy would bring me sometimes. Then Daddy Waters would let me come with him sometimes. Strange thing, that top up there always gave me the creeps."

"Just an old mountaintop," his cousin, Linda, said, turning to feel the cool of a mountain breeze wafting up the hollow to where they both sat on a fallen tree trunk, enjoying the late-autumn day.

A whining sound came from the mountaintop, which was dipped in somewhat. No trees grew there.

"Has it been clear cut?" Linda asked, noticing all the big hardwood timber in the hollow below. "Is that why it's so creepy? It does look out of place with that big dip at the top, instead of going on up like all the rest of the tops around here."

"The dip is called a saddle," Richard answered. "I don't think it's ever had the timber cut anywhere here. Well, not in our lifetime anyway."

The wind picked up, sounding almost like a horse whinnying as it whisked up the mountainside. Linda shivered even though the day was warm.

"Why is it called Mule Mountain?" she asked.

Richard knew his cousin would not like the answer. He twisted a piece of broken twig between his thumb and forefinger as the wind whinnied again. He'd heard the sound many times, and it never failed to raise the hair on the back of his neck.

"Well?" Linda asked again, giving the man beside her an impatient stare.

Richard sighed, then said, "The locals used to bring their horses and mules and maybe cows, too, up there, up there in the saddle, to shoot them."

"What?" Linda gasped. Then, believing her cousin was making up a tall story, added, "No pigs? Why didn't the people bring their pigs, too?"

"Serious," he said, peeling the bark away from the twig. "A long time ago, most of the area around here was pasture or fields. People lived off the land, and animals were always getting sick—too sick to get better—or dying of old age. Somebody found this place. It seemed the perfect place, not too close to the settlement and not too far away from it, to dispose of animals."

Linda stared at Richard, knowing he was telling the truth but not wanting to believe it. "So cruel," she thought.

"You can't just shoot a mule anywhere," the man said, trying to explain the reality of their ancestors' situation. "You have to bury them. And up here, in the saddle, they just walked the animals down in the low spot and shot them and left them there."

"Did they dig a grave or anything?" Linda asked, still shocked by the story she heard.

"No," came the answer. "They just left them. Nature took care of the remains."

"That's terrible," the woman said.

"No, it's not," Richard interrupted before Linda could get all worked up. "Animals lay where they fall in the wild. Nature recycles its own."

"But this wasn't natural," she said.

"But the animals' dying was inevitable, and their owners were maybe being kinder by their actions. And they didn't have time to bury something that big. Do you have any idea of how big a hole that would take? And to dig it with a shovel?"

Linda didn't say anything, trying to see the logic. Then, swiping a tangle of hair away from her face, she asked, "You ever been up there?"

Richard nodded. "Just a pile of old bones," he said. "Lots of old bones."

The wind whinnied again, echoing long and sending bone-chilling cold through the cousins. The twosome stood as the hair prickled on the backs of their necks. They hurried to be away from the place where the wind sounded as a reminder of the animals who came to the mountaintop but did not leave. Perhaps their spirits were still there, running up and around the mountain. Running and running in the wind on Mule Mountain.

Ghost at the Lake

MR. PHILHOWER COULD NOT TELL A ghost story. Ask him about computers and he would regale one with tales of megabytes, Windows, and hard-drive crashes. He taught computer science at the Tech School. His assistant on this camping trip for underprivileged city boys was Joe Dugan, a policeman. Well, Joe was better at teaching kids to swim.

The campers were near the Tennessee-North Carolina border. The nearest town of any size was Murphy, and the boys never got that far to the east. The boys swam and fished and did all the good things campers do.

The youngsters thought the nightly campfires, with darkness approaching and strange noises coming from deep in the forest, would provide a perfect opportunity to hear some ghost stories. Alas, that was not to be, for both men stuttered and ruined whatever pathetic ghost tales they tried to tell.

One of the highlights of each day was a half-mile hike to Pa's Country Store, the only place the few inhabitants of the isolated area had to get their staples. On the third day of their week-long outing, the boys piled into Pa's for an ice-cream bar and a bottle of soda pop.

"Mr. Philhower," one of the boys asked after they had finished their treats, "why don't you see if Pa knows anyone to tell us some ghost stories?"

"Good idea," said Mr. Philhower, pushing up the glasses that were always slipping down his nose. "Pa, do you know anyone who can tell these boys some ghost stories?"

"Well, not offhand," said Pa. "But I'll ask around. Maybe someone will come in this afternoon."

It was just before dark that same evening, and as the boys roasted marshmallows, a tall, well-dressed young man walked into the campsite.

"Are you the fellows who need someone to tell a few ghost stories?" he asked, speaking in a dignified matter, almost like an Englishman.

"Yes, we are. I'm Harold Philhower and this is Joe Dugan. And we desperately need someone to tell some ghost stories for the boys."

"My name is John Blue, and I'll try to entertain them," the man said. He told a couple of ghostly tales, and the boy's eyes seemed to widen with each word.

The evening grew dark and cloudy, and there was no moonlight.

"And now," said Blue, "I'll tell you my favorite ghost tale." The woods became darker and seemed spookier than ever.

"My story," he began, "happened a long time ago. It must have been over fifty years ago, and it was right across the lake from where we are now. There stood a mansion— it was the Howard summer place—and rich people came all summer and gala parties were the order of the day."

"Whoo? Whoo?" asked an owl. The boys moved closer together, and even Mr. Philhower and Joe leaned forward to hear their guest.

"Let's see, there were old man Howard, his wife, and their debutante daughter, Laurel. Oh, she was something, a real beauty, and she had just broken off her engagement to a young man, a stockbroker. Laurel had met another man, and her fiancé took it real hard. He would call at all hours of the day and night. He even threatened the Howards. It was in late spring and the Howards decided to come up here to get away from the man with the broken heart."

The campfire flickered and burned low as all eyes were on John Blue.

"Old man Howard," he continued, "heard that Laurel's ex had followed them up here to the lake. The sheriff was notified, and he sent two deputies to check out the Howard place, but they arrived too late. When the deputies drove up the driveway, they saw the mansion was engulfed in flames. They called in the volunteer fire department, but they knew it was useless. There was no sign that anyone had survived the holocaust. The Howards never had a chance.

" 'Hey look!' yelled one of the officers. 'There's someone running toward the lake.' Both lawmen gave chase, yelling, 'Stop in the name of the law!' But the figure kept running. He reached the shoreline, then turned and laughed an insane laugh.

"Then the man, whom both deputies later identified as the jilted suitor, walked into the lake. The sheriff's men shouted, 'Stop or we'll shoot!' But he kept going into the water. Shots were fired. Both lawmen said they hit the man and that he fell into the lake.

"The sheriff arrived with more men, and they searched throughout the night but to no avail. They never found the body of Laurel Howard's ex-fiancé, nor was he ever seen again. Folks around here say the lake's still haunted by that terrible murderer."

That was Blue's final ghost story of the night, and everyone thanked him before he left. The campfire soon burned down and the boys went to bed.

The next afternoon, when the campers were at Pa's having their treats, Mr. Philhower said, "Say, Pa, that was a pretty good ghost-story teller you sent to us."

"Oh?" said Pa. "What did he say his name was?"

"John Blue," answered Philhower.

"Well, son," said Pa, "I never sent anyone to tell you any ghost stories. And if he said his name was John Blue—well, John Blue was the fellow that burned down the Howard place. Seems he was jilted by the young Howard girl, and—" Mr. Philhower gathered his charges and left before Pa could finish.

If anyone wants to know about computers, just ask Mr. Philhower. But don't ever ask him about ghosts or ghost stories.

VIRGINIA'S GHOST

"IT'S THE STRANGEST THING," SAID Virginia, a young mother of two. "I never really thought about ghosts until we moved to the house south of town. I knew as soon as we moved in there was something unusual, but I just couldn't put a name to it.

"I put the baby in the bedroom by the front door and every time someone rang the doorbell she woke up. So, I put a sign on the door that read: PLEASE DON'T RING DOORBELL—BABY IS SLEEPING."

A smile graced the young woman s lips as she continued, "As soon as the sign was hung, the doorbell stopped working and didn't work again, even after the sign was removed. Two years later, when the baby was moved to another room—that very day after my daughter was settled and all her belongings removed—the doorbell mysteriously began working again.

"There were also other telltale signs of an unseen visitor. The commodes in the bathrooms would flush by themselves at the oddest times, when no one was in there. And lights would mysteriously turn on and off, usually when my husband was out of town.

"But, this ghost never made any trouble or gave us cause to be afraid. I believe it was there to watch over us and keep us safe. Later, when we sold the house, it stayed.

"We live in the perfect place now, here with the hills and mountains in the far reaches of Clayton County. I suppose most ghosts would be comfortable here, but our ghost preferred the house in the suburbs. I wonder if it still walks the halls, checking on the occupants and seeing that all requests are carried out."

SÉANCE

TEENAGERS HERE IN THE SOUTHERN Appalachian foothills are like most teenagers anywhere. They look for excitement and adventure and sometimes discover more than they bargained for. Such was the case of two young girls left home alone when one girl's parents went out for the evening.

The girls were instructed not to leave the house or invite any of their friends over while the parents were out. The girls agreed to be on their best behavior and smiled as they promised.

The girls, both fourteen years old, watched television for a while, then listened to records and ate junk food. But as the night grew long, they became bored. Somehow the subject of ancestors came up, and because the grandmother of one of the girls had recently died, they decided to hold a séance.

"We were just going to fool around," said Jodi, "you know, see if we could get any vibes. I thought I might even shake the table a little and scare my friend, Cathy. After all it was her idea, her house, and it was her grandmother we were going to try and reach."

Jodi gave a little nervous laugh then continued.

"We got a bell, and a Bible, and half a candle. Cathy read somewhere those were the things we would need. Then, for a personal item, we used her grandmother's shawl. Cathy said her mother had kept it because it was her grandmother's favorite. I think maybe the grand- mother may have even crocheted it herself.

"I knew Cathy's grandmother. She always was su- perstitious and believed in ghosts and haunts and all that supernatural stuff. So we decided if anybody would come to us, it would be her.

"We laid the shawl out across the small dining room table then placed the candle in the middle and the bell and Bible out to the sides. We sat down across from one another to practice. Each of us reached and touched both the bell and the Bible. The candle sat in the center of our circle.

"I was beginning to feel a little strange, but it was just going to be fun."

Jodi stopped talking and rubbed a shaky hand through her short blond hair. Then, placing delicate hands on her slim hips, she continued. "We were just kids, delving into black magic or something. It still makes me shake when I think back about it.

"Well, anyway, when we decided we were ready, Cathy lit the candle and I turned off the lights and we took our places, forming the circle around the lit candle. It was dark as pitch everywhere except right there in that little circle of light. It was eerie. Then Cathy starting call- ing out for her grandmother. I laughed and she did, too.

"Then we got serious and closed our eyes. Cathy called again and everything was so quiet. Nothing. Cathy called three more times, and the last time she called, the cat yowled like the hounds of hell had him. We opened our eyes and quickly turned to see a ball of light floating on the stairs. The cat was at the bottom of the stairs and every hair on him was turned backward.

"Every hair on me stood up, too, and I was ice-cold to the bone.

"Cathy screamed. The candle flickered and went out. The light on the stairs just hovered, floating or something. I don't know how I did it, but I got the lights turned back on. There was nothing there on the stairs, just the cat, growling and his eyes blazing in fear, still crouched at the bottom of the steps.

"Neither Cathy nor I said anything; we just moved the stuff off the table as fast as we could.

"The room had turned a chilling cold, so we huddled together on the couch in the living room under her grandmother's shawl until her parents came home and everyone went upstairs to bed.

"I don't know what we conjured up that night, if we even conjured up anything at all. I just remember the cold cutting through and through, the floating light on the stairs, and the cat in some kind of terrorized state.

"It's been years since that took place, and to this day neither Cathy nor myself has ever broached the subject of that séance to the other. I guess some things are best just not talked about lest we stir them up again."

THE MAN
WHO HATED FLOWERS

MABLE AARON HAS LIVED HERE IN THE Appalachian foothill mountains all her life. She raised her children, watched her grandchildren grow up, and now enjoys her great-grandchildren. She has seen and heard things in her living that most people would never believe. But her mind is clear and her memories ripe for the telling.

There was an old man, living in the long-ago settlement, who detested flowers and forbade his wife to even have a flower garden. He said her time was better spent elsewhere. Besides, since they didn't really serve a purpose as food, clothing, or shelter, he thought flower gardens were a foolish waste and misuse of the soil.

The old man always "hmmphed" when flowers were mentioned around him, and he scowled at the custom of placing flowers on graves.

When the old man died, he was laid out at his home because there were no funeral parlors at the time. For whatever reason, all who died got flowers, even if they were against flowers, like the old man was. Relatives and neighbors brought food and any flowers that were available. Sometimes folks made flowers from colored paper dipped in hot wax. It was also customary for the visitors to stay with the family until the funeral took place. That's just the way things were done at the time.

But every time someone would go into the mourning room, where the old man's body lay, the flowers would be on the floor. No matter how many times the flowers were picked up and placed back on the coffin, they wound up on the floor again.

Even in death, the old man hated flowers and would have his feelings known.

COURTSHIP

COURTSHIP IN SOUTHERN APPALACHIA IS a normal thing. It is almost always the same: Boy meets girl, boy calls on girl and girl's family, and marriage takes place soon after.

The courtship of George and Emmy had a slightly different twist. For one thing, Emmy and her family lived on a farm that had been in the family for generations. George, however, was a city boy. He came to the mountains on vacation and stayed at the summer hotel. It was love at first sight, at least for George, and all who saw them together nodded and said they were a perfect match. Of course, the people who said that were city folks staying at the hotel. Emmy fretted about telling her folks about George, a city man.

They met the summer Emmy worked at the five-and-dime in town. Every evening after Emmy got off work, George would walk her down the river to a small bridge. There, holding hands, they would say good night. Then Emmy would cross the bridge and they'd walk back the way they had come, Emmy on one side of the river and George on the other. One night while on opposite sides of the river, George yelled, "Emmy, I love you."

Emmy, her heart almost bursting with joy, ran all the way home. At supper that night she made an announcement: "I got a beau."

Mama said, "You'll have to bring him to supper. We want to get a look at him."

Pa said, "Hmmph!"

Her two younger brothers made plans for when Emmy's beau came to meet the family.

Two nights later George was invited to supper. He didn't walk Emmy down to the bridge. She was off work that day.

"Emmy," said George, "I'm not going to walk all the way down to the bridge and then walk all the way back to your folks' place. I'll be all sweaty, so I'll rent a boat and cross farther up, and it will be a shorter walk."

Emmy drew a map and said, "You won't have any trouble finding the place. Just walk up the path from the river. It's only half a mile to our farm, and we are the only place on the road. There's an old house down by the river, but nobody has lived there for years."

Everything went smoothly. George banked the boat, walked up the path, turned right, and in no time at all was walking up the front yard of Emmy's house.

She ran out to meet him and they hugged, which wasn't exactly proper, but Mama just nodded.

After supper they all sat in the parlor. Mama lit the oil lamps, and George told about his family and his prospects.

"I'm going to buy the dry goods store in town, and I'd like to marry Emmy," he said.

Emmy blushed.

Mama sighed.

Pa said, "Hmmph!"

Earl and Pete, the brothers, winked at each other.

And so it was settled. George and Emmy would marry.

"Hey Pa," said Earl, "tell George about the Moore place and the ghost."

"Now you young'uns hush up," said Mama.

"No, that's all right, Mrs. Samuels," said George. "I like ghost stories." Of course, George, being on his best behavior and in love, would have listened to anything.

"Hmmph," said Pa, and began. "The old Moore place is not quite half a mile from here. In fact, it's almost on the river, just up from where you banked your boat. There's a path, but it's overgrown now with briers and the like. Anyway, old Tom Moore, he was a rich city fellow, built a house on the river, a big house. Now when I was a boy, him and Mrs. Moore were nice folks, but they didn't socialize much. Oh, every Labor Day they'd have a picnic for the locals, and we all went."

Pa paused, took a sip of coffee, and continued. "Now when me and Mama got hitched, we became quite friendly with the Moores. We'd go to their place for supper, and they'd come here to our place. Mrs. Moore was a gardener, and boy, did she have a garden. It was the biggest and best I had ever seen. Then just like that, Mrs. Moore up and died. Old Tom was heartbroken. Then he got strange. He wouldn't let anyone near his house. If a body so much as looked at the garden, he'd come running out and chase them away.

"Well, old Tom died about twenty years ago, and since then, folks who wander onto the Moore property swear some old coot comes roaring out and chases them or scares them off.

"Pure poppycock," said Pa. "I don't believe it, but that's our ghost story."

Soon it was time for George to go. Emmy walked him down to the road and they shared their first kiss. George started back to where he left the boat. There was no moon and it was pitch dark. "I couldn't believe it could get that dark," George said later.

Then lightning began to flash, followed by thunder, and George began to move faster. It seemed he'd walked five miles already. Lightning again seared across the blackened night.

"That old ghost story didn't scare me," said George bravely.

Again lightning lit up the night, and there was the path to the river. As George turned down the path, it seemed to him that the dark night had brought out dozens of bushes. Up ahead he saw an old house, more like a mansion, really. George could swear he smelled the scent of flowers. Lightning lit up the entire area, and George saw an old man loping toward him, carrying a club and screaming curses.

George turned and flew back up the path, skidding to a stop only when he reached the dirt road. He found the right path, then ran to the river and his boat.

On George and Emmy's fiftieth anniversary, George told the tale of his encounter with a ghost. He laughed and said, "Those rascals Pete and Earl set the whole thing up. One of them dressed up like old Tom Moore."

After George left the room, Emmy said, "It wasn't Earl or Pete that George saw that night. They never left the house. When George left, we played cards to almost midnight."

Emmy winked and said, "George really did see a ghost that night, but we're not ever going to tell him he did."

ALICE'S FRIEND

ALICE MARTIN WAS SICK, BAD SICK. SHE lived with her husband, Michael, in the mountains of eastern Kentucky. Alice was so sick that Michael insisted she go to the new doctor in town.

The doctor checked Alice over and said, "Mrs. Martin, I'm going to give you two prescriptions, one for the fever and one for pain."

After getting the prescriptions filled at the local drugstore, Michael said, "I'm going to make sure you take your medicine. I'm going to give them to you just like it says on the bottle, four times a day, four pills each time."

Michael had a job of sorts and left home every morning after giving Alice her medicine. He would come home at lunchtime, give Alice her pills, then leave until dark. He would give her pills when he got home and before he went to bed.

Alice's condition did not improve. In fact, she got weaker and weaker. She got so weak she couldn't get out of bed even to bathe.

One afternoon after Michael had left, Alice heard a knock on the door. "Come in," she said weakly.

"Hello, Mrs. Martin," said the woman as she entered. "My name is Alissa. I met your husband in the drugstore. He said it would be all right if I came to sit with you a bit."

As sick as Alice was, Alissa's voice seemed to pick her up. They chatted a bit, then Alissa said, "I have to go now, but I'll be back tomorrow and I'll give you a bath. Oh, Alice, don't say anything about me being here. My husband is an old fuddy-duddy."

"Where do you live?" asked Alice.

"I live off Old Mine Road up in the holler. Well, good-bye for now. I'll see you tomorrow."

Alice knew where her new friend lived since she had often walked about the countryside while growing up. Funny, she didn't remember anyone ever living there, at least not in her lifetime.

It wasn't ten minutes after Michael left the next morning that Alissa arrived at Alice's home.

"Now you just let me take you in there and give you a bath," Alissa said.

After the bath Alice felt a little better, but she was still so weak.

On Alissa's fourth visit, she asked, "Alice, where is your medicine? I'd like to take a look at it."

"My husband has it. He says I won't take it if he doesn't give it to me."

"Alice," said Alissa, "I won't be back anymore. But there is one more thing that I have to tell you."

"What's that?" asked Alice, sorry to be losing her new friend. Funny, she had never noticed how familiar Alissa looked.

"It's your husband," said Alissa. "He's trying to kill you. He's giving you too much medicine."

"But why?" moaned Alice.

"Because of this property your daddy left you. It's valuable and your husband wants to sell it."

"But what will I do?"

"Don't worry, Alice. I have to go now, but help is on the way." And with that, Alissa left.

The next afternoon Alice knew she was through. She would never last out the night. She sobbed, "I'm too young to die."

Then the front door burst open, and a formidable figure strolled in.

"Aunt Maggie," gasped Alice. "Oh, help me."

Now in most southern Appalachian families there is one person who rules the family. No one would dare argue with the Aunt Maggies, because the Aunt Maggies are always right. Alice's Aunt Maggie lived in Lexington, and why she should be in her niece's home she couldn't rightly say—only she had a premonition, and there she was.

"Come on, Alice, I'm taking you to your doctor. Oh, who is your doctor?"

"It's Dr. Wright. He's new in town."

Aunt Maggie bundled up Alice, carried her out to the car, and sped to the small town and the doctor's office.

The doctor took one look at Alice and asked, "Haven't you been taking your medicine?"

"Yes, I have, just like you said. My husband gives them to me. Four each, four times a day."

"What!" yelled Doctor Wright.

"Yes," said Alice. "I never saw the bottles the pills came in. And my friend, Alissa, says Michael, my husband, is trying to kill me."

Dr. Wright made two phone calls. The first was to the pharmacist, who verified that Michael had filled the prescriptions. The second call was to the sheriff.

Alice was taken to a hospital in Lexington where she recovered her health and was soon released.

Later, Dr. Wright asked the sheriff, "Are you going to arrest Alice Martin's husband?"

"No," answered the sheriff, "we don't have enough to hold him. But he's gone and won't be back here. Alice has started divorce action against Michael Martin, and she will get it.

"Funny thing, though. We went out to Old Mine Road. You know, where that friend of Alice said she lived? Well, there's nobody living out there. There's an old cabin, but it's flat on the ground."

The sheriff paused, then added, "What's really funny is, Michael Martin denied he'd ever heard of an Alissa. And he vehemently denied that he ever sent her or anyone else to sit with Alice. And you know something, Doc? I believe him. I think Alice Martin conjured up an apparition or something. Maybe Alissa is really Alice. Who can say? But I don't think we'll ever know for sure."

THE SHADOWMAN

THE DRIVER'S SIDE SEAT BELT ON HER CAR had not been functioning properly for quite a while. Sometimes it wouldn't open. Other times Marlene could not get it to stay closed. Unfortunately, she could never tell what the thing would do until she tried to get out of it. Still, she snapped it shut and hoped it would hold fast, not really concerned. She'd never had a serious accident before, and she didn't expect to begin today.

Tina, Marlene's daughter, sat in the backseat of the car. Tina was seven and still played with dolls. She was talking to one of her "babies" in a low, cooing voice. Marlene glanced back at her daughter, then looked up at the house.

It was an ordinary house in a quiet neighborhood. The houses next door and across the street were similar in design, just basic ranch-style houses, nothing extraordinary. At least that was the way it looked from the outside. On the inside Marlene knew it was a different story.

Marlene knew something was odd about the house the moment she walked through the kitchen door, and it had nothing to do with the fact that the house had sat empty for more than a year. It had to do with the way light and shadow played against the walls, especially in the room Marlene shared with her husband, Joe.

A week after the family moved into the house Marlene saw the shadow of a man sitting in her chair in the bedroom. She didn't let herself think it was real, not at first. Before she called it a shadow and accepted that it was the shadow of a man, Marlene tried to find the source of the dark silhouette.

Marlene tried closing the curtains at night. Still the shadow remained. She tried opening the curtains to varying degrees. It remained. She closed the door to the hall. It remained. She moved the chair to other parts of the room. The shadow traveled with the chair, no matter where Marlene put it. Finally, she asked her husband if he saw the shadow. To her relief, he did. In fact, everyone saw the shadow, including seven-year-old Tina.

That her young daughter saw the shadow as well frightened Marlene at first. What would she do, she wondered, if the source of the shadow was evil and actually hurt Tina? But somehow, Marlene had never thought the shadowman was evil, nor had she ever been afraid of it. No one in the family was. They grew so comfortable with the shadowman that they began to call it George.

Marlene thought about all these things as she backed the car down the driveway and headed out of the neighborhood. She often found herself thinking about the shadowman at odd times of the day, like while she was shopping or waiting in the dentist's office or driving Tina to a visit with friends. Even now, Marlene felt the presence of the shadowman in the car with her, though she realized it was probably only her imagination.

Lately, she had considered getting rid of the chair where the shadow sat. Though she thought it a comfortable chair, to be sure, it didn't quite fit in with what she wanted to do in decorating the bedroom. Besides, she'd bought the chair secondhand at a thrift shop when she and Joe first married, so she wasn't exactly attached to it, not like the few bits and pieces from both sets of parents.

But she was reluctant to get rid of the chair because she didn't really want George to go.

Marlene couldn't remember the times she had been home alone and gotten some sort of fright over noises outside or down in the basement. Once a convict escaped and she rushed around the house locking doors and windows, but something had told her she would be fine, that nothing bad would happen to her. She would become calm, and all her fears would just melt away.

As Marlene headed out into heavier traffic, she forgot about home and concentrated on driving instead. Absently, she checked her seat belt and, finding that the buckle had not held, looked down as she tried to adjust it. She did not see the pickup truck cutting across traffic until it was too late to do anything. Then everything seemed to slow down, and Marlene saw things in terrible, terrible detail. And all she could think of was Tina in the backseat.

Later, the accident report would say that Marlene's seat belt had come unbuckled, that the impact of the pickup truck hitting her car drove her into the steering wheel and caused her to hit her head on the windshield, and that it was the other driver's fault.

What the report did not say was that Marlene had seen a shadow in her car and felt an arm holding her back. And it could not say why Marlene was so calm after the accident. Nor could it tell anyone why the shadowman was not in his chair that evening when Joe brought Marlene and Tina home from the emergency room—or why the shadow has not returned since.

MOTHER MOREHILL

FOR GENERATIONS THE MOREHILLS LIVED in and around the Appalachian foothills of Braxton County. There were times when one would move away looking for work or perhaps marry someone not of the area, but after maybe a year or two, the wanderer always returned not too far from his or her original earthen roots. They were family rooted, too, like most folks in the foothills.

But Bertha Morehill Elder was rooted a little deeper than most, especially with her brother married and he and his wife, Belinda, raising children and grandchildren of their own on the other side of the county. The brother visited his mother and sister often. He brought groceries and gifts to both women, but Mr. Morehill, Bertha's father, had left his family well provided for, so their needs and most of their wants were readily met.

Bertha was a true blessing to the Morehill household and took her responsibilities very seriously. Being the youngest, she always felt herself to be special. Bertha spent most of her adult life looking after her widowed, sickly mother. She was regarded highly in the community because of the sacrifices she had made.

Some of the old-timers even said the woman had turned down a proposal of marriage from a traveling preacher when she sadly realized she would have to take on the duties of a preacher's wife and minister to total strangers and leave the ministering of her mother to someone who might be a stranger.

Bertha was said to be "good as gold" to the woman who gave birth to her. She was never heard to say an unkind word or commit any unkind act toward Mrs. Morehill during their lifetime together.

Everyone who knew them grieved for both mother and daughter when the old woman died at age ninety-three, leaving sixty-one-year-old Bertha to face the world alone.

A great-niece, Alice, visited Bertha on a regular basis and discovered that Bertha always included her mother in their conversations, even asking the dead woman questions. It seemed that all aspects of Bertha's life still revolved around her mother, even though the woman had been dead and buried for more than two years.

"Well," said Bertha, when Alice asked why she carried on so, "I guess maybe 'cause it's just always been Mother and myself that I know she's still here. She even finds things I've lost and puts them on the night table. No, dear, I'm not crazy as you might suspect. I've still got control of all my faculties."

A few months later when Alice visited, Bertha informed her great-niece that she and the newly widowed Mr. Robert Elder, owner of the dry goods store, were to be married.

Alice was quite shaken by the announcement and questioned her great-aunt Bertha rather severely.

"What about moving?" asked Alice.

"No, dear, we'll live here," came the answer. "His children are all grown, and this house is large enough for the two of us."

"What about Grandmama Morehill? Does Mr. Elder know about her?" Alice inquired skeptically.

"Of course, child," the older woman huffed. "He's been to Sunday dinner three times."

"And . . . and Grandmama Morehill?" Alice stuttered. "What does she think of this marriage to Mr. Elder?"

"She approves."

"She approves? How do you know for sure?" the younger woman pleaded.

"Because, Alice, she left her wedding band there on the night table the day after I told her about Mr. Elder's proposal," Bertha said with a blushing smile.

TRAVELING MAN

WHEN ELIZABETH GROVER WAS A LITTLE girl growing up in East Tennessee, she and her younger sister, Lily, were playing in the front yard one day. Their mother, Jennie, was watching them while she shelled peas. Suddenly, Lily started screaming and pointed across the road from their house.

Jennie asked, "Lily, what's the matter?"

But Lily continued to scream and point across the road.

"There's a scary-looking man over there," Lily cried.

"Elizabeth," said Jennie, "you stay with your sister while I go over and see what's scaring Lily."

When she returned, Jennie said, "There's nothing over there, and there's no sign of anyone."

Now the place across the road had many briers and ugly, twisted trees, but there was no place a person or animal could hide. They all went back into their cabin, and Jennie consoled Lily. After a bit Granny Grover came to visit and was told that Lily had seen something strange.

"Well, years ago," said Granny, "there was a large oak tree over there. And one night some men hung a criminal, at least they said he was a criminal. After the man was cut down and buried, we had a terrible storm. I remember all us children hiding under the covers. The next day we all went outside, and darned if that big old oak tree hadn't been hit by lightning. It was spilt right down the middle, and both sides lay on the ground."

It was exactly one week after Lily's experience that Cousin Bert, who was about twenty-five and a favorite of Lily and the rest of the children, stopped by. Bert stayed for supper and afterward, as he prepared to leave, everyone went to the front door to see him off.

Bert walked out onto the road, stopped, and yelled, "Look at that man he's . . . he's evil looking!"

Everyone looked but saw no one. Bert ran across the road and onto the property. He looked like he was chasing someone and kept yelling, "Hold on there, mister! Why are you going around scaring kids?"

About a hour later Papaw and Uncle Fred went looking for Bert, but they couldn't find him. Bert didn't come back that night, and the next day the two men went back to search again, while Jennie, Lily, and Elizabeth went to get the sheriff. The girls and their mother returned with the sheriff and two deputies, who went across the road where Papaw and Uncle Fred were searching.

About two hours later they came back with Bert's body and sent for the coroner.

"It looks like Bert froze to death," the sheriff said to the coroner. "He's all curled up and stiff as a board. Oh, one more thing," the sheriff continued, "the ground was all chewed up like he was in pain. No, it was more like he clawed the ground around him."

"Well, for one thing," the coroner said, "it didn't get below fifty degrees last night so Bert couldn't have froze."

Elizabeth learned later that the official verdict was that Bert had died of a heart attack. The coroner later told Uncle Fred unofficially that Bert died because he was literally scared to death by someone, or something, unexplainable.

JACK

ANIMALS ARE SAID TO HAVE KEENER *senses than humans. They are also said to have an extra sense that is tuned in to yet another level of being. Maybe that explains why people of the Appalachian foothills developed such attachments to their animals in times past. It has been reported many times through the years that the family dog has saved its owners from burning houses, warned of coming destructive storms, and even gone for help when one of its humans was in trouble.*

George Johnson had a little mongrel dog named Jack. The dog went everywhere his master did. They were indeed fine friends. Then George got sick and had to go to the hospital. During his stay at the facility, George's daughter, Ruth, took care of Jack.

One Sunday morning Ruth saw Jack on her back porch where her own dog, Mitzi, lay sleeping. Jack suddenly stared down the road in the direction of his master's house and began to howl. It was a slow, mournful noise that disturbed Ruth. She'd often heard folks talk of dogs howling "The Death Song" if death was near to a family member.

Ruth hurried outside and persuaded the dog to hush, but as soon as she returned inside, the little dog went out into the driveway, peered toward his master's house, and began again to howl.

Mitzi never awoke from her sleeping on the porch.

George came home from the hospital a few days later, but the family was told he would never get well. Jack stayed close by George's bed for several days, leaving only to eat and relieve himself. Then one day, he didn't come back in after being let out. Since the dog would never wear a collar, it was thought that a passerby had picked him up along the highway, believing him to be a stray.

George died two weeks later, and the family mourned his death and the loss of Jack, who had been so much a part of the old man's life.

Three or four days after the funeral, Ruth heard a whining sound outside the back door. It wasn't Mitzi. Ruth opened the door and found Jack standing there. He came inside reluctantly, and Ruth fed and watered him and called her mother to report that Jack had returned. The two women cried, glad that the little dog had found his way back to them.

A short time later, Ruth took the dog out so he could go home. Jack sat down in the driveway, looked toward his master's house, and whined. No matter how much Ruth coaxed, the dog wouldn't go home.

The next day, Ruth and her mother went to the cemetery to clean off George's grave. Jack went too.

The little dog sat beside the grave until all the dead and wilted flowers were removed, then lay down lengthways on the top of the grave and whined. Jack stayed there as if in a state of mourning while the women took the old flowers to a designated area outside the cemetery to dispose of them.

When the women returned, Jack climbed back into the car. As soon as Ruth drove into the yard of her parents' house and opened the car door, the little dog jumped out and ran to the porch. It was as though he knew George was gone now, but with that knowing, Jack was ready to look after those of his human family who remained.

THE ROAD LESS TRAVELED

"OH, SAY, RIGHT AFTER THE KOREAN War," began Wilma Griggs, "we had two friends of my brother Sam staying with us for the summer. We lived in western Gilmer County then, and they stayed in the cabin down by the old dirt road. That road is paved now. They were friends of Sam's from college and were both schoolteachers. Their names were Mark and Cliff. They had both brought bicycles and they rode all over the county.

"One day they decided to follow the old dirt road around the mountain. Usually, they took the right fork, but that day they went to the left. Now today that road is all grown up, but back then it was still passable.

"The first time they took the left fork, Mark got a flat tire just as they passed the old Willows Plantation. The plantation was long gone; only a pile of rocks remained of the once-grand home. So they came back, with Mark pushing his bicycle. Two days later they pedaled off, and as they were passing the old plantation, Cliff's tire went flat, so back they came."

Wilma smiled as she continued her tale. "The teachers decided to run into the county seat and get a couple of bicycle repair kits. They really didn't need them, because when they got back to their cabin, they couldn't find anything wrong with the tires.

"Once more, and for the last time, the two teachers pedaled around the mountain, and do you know, when they got to the plantation ruins, they both got flat tires.

"Mark said he was pumping up his tire when Cliff said, 'Mark, look over there by that pile of rocks.' Mark looked, and there stood a man dressed in clothes that folks wore in the last century. He wore a straw hat and had a straw stuck in his teeth.

"Cliff said, 'Hello there!' But the man never answered.

"Both Mark and Cliff started walking toward the man. They thought he was a young man, about their age. The man paid no attention to the teachers.

" 'Hello,' said Mark. 'Nice day.' But the man seemed to look right through them. They came within ten feet of the strange man. 'Good morning, sir,' Mark said.

"The man turned toward the teachers, chewed the straw between his teeth, and disappeared. They searched high and low but never found a sign of anyone.

"The young men came back to our place and finished out the summer but never went back to the plantation. Later they found out from a local historian that many years ago the owner of the plantation had murdered his son right in front of where the manor stood."

DREAMS

THE HOUSE WAS NOT HAUNTED BY A ghost. It wasn't really haunted, not in the strictest sense of the word. What happened in the house was just unusual.

On a Sunday in 1941 the family that eventually built the house sat down in their living room and spread out the plans on the floor. The radio was on, and the parents and their children contributed to the noise by having a lively discussion about what the new house should be like. They had saved money for its construction and, though war had overrun Europe and threatened the United States, they expected to break ground early in the new year. But it was December 7, and a place few had ever heard of had been bombed by the Japanese. Pearl Harbor and World War II delayed the construction of the house for over two years.

When the house was eventually built, everything went well. The framing lumber was milled locally, and more than one old-timer pronounced that the house was so well built it could withstand a tornado.

For years the family thrived there. On warm evenings the family, which included grandchildren and soon some great-grandchildren, would sit on the porch, talk in low voices, and watch the young ones catch fire-flies and put them in jars. But the father grew older and older and more tired, until one day he passed away and the mother was left alone.

At first the daughters took turns spending nights with their mother. That hardly worked well. They had homes and families of their own, and it's difficult to spend a couple of nights a week away from one's own bed. Soon they hired a granddaughter to spend nights with their mother, and this was the arrangement for five years.

"You'd think I would have been afraid in that house," Catherine, the granddaughter, said. "It was right on a heavily traveled road. It had one of those semicircle driveways, and people were always pulling in to turn around. There were no locks on the windows, and the doors only had latches. We always sat in the den, and you couldn't hear a thing because the den was at the back of the house away from the front door. But except for a few times when I'd seen a spooky movie or read a book of ghost stories, I was never afraid."

Though it had received a few improvements since its construction in the forties, the house was basically the same. You walked up onto the front porch and into a large living room. To the left was a dining room, and to the right was a bedroom with a closed-in carport that was used as storage. Straight ahead was a door into a small hallway. Off the hallway was another bedroom, a bath that was once a bedroom before indoor plumbing, and a den to the left. From the den one could see another bed-room and the kitchen. Off the kitchen was an enclosed back porch housing the dryer and well pump.

"When I stayed," Catherine continued, "a couple of my cousins would sometimes stay with me. They would sleep in the den on a bed right in the middle of the room. I had the bedroom off the hallway, next to the bathroom.

"One night when they stayed with me, the elder had a friend staying as well. That night I went to bed first, closed the door to my room so they wouldn't disturb me if they decided to talk, and drifted off into a very deep sleep. Sometime during that night I had a dream, but it was one of those very vivid dreams where every detail is sharp and clear.

"I dreamed that I got out of bed, the very bed I was in, took the time to put house shoes on, and walked down the hall into the den. Once there I looked around, checking on my cousins and their friend. I took note of where everyone was sleeping, I looked to see if our grandmother was all right in her bedroom off the den, then I went back to my bed.

"In my dream the elder cousin and her friend were asleep on the iron bed. The younger cousin was asleep on the couch. This was not unusual. The friend was the elder cousin's guest, after all. What was unusual was that the two girls were sleeping with their heads toward the foot of the bed.

"When I got up the next morning, I packed up my things and prepared to go home. Like in the dream, I checked on the girls and my grandmother. And like in the dream, my younger cousin was asleep on the couch and the other two girls were asleep in the bed with their heads to the foot of the bed. I had no way of knowing this beforehand because I had gone to bed first.

"You're probably thinking I walk in my sleep," Catherine said, a serious expression on her face. "I don't walk or talk in my sleep; I barely move. So how did I know how the girls were arranged in sleep—right down to which side of the bed they slept on? I don't know, but that wasn't the last unusual dream I had in the house."

Catherine stayed with her grandmother at night for more than four years, and during that time she felt a certain sense of security in the house that she could not explain. It was as if someone, or something, was in the house protecting its occupants. One morning that something warned Catherine of a serious accident already in the making.

The old house had little insulation. In the fall, when the days could be very warm and the nights freezing, Catherine's aunts and uncles were reluctant to light the gas heater. Why heat up the little house during the day, when one could throw on an extra blanket at night to cut the chill? But Catherine's grandmother was beyond such reasoning. She had turned ninety that year, and when she was cold, she was cold and wanted heat.

"Again, I was asleep," Catherine continued. "Asleep and having a vivid dream about the house. I was lying in bed and I could see everything in the room. It was exact in detail, right down to the blue, gray, and burgundy horse blankets over the windows.

"The window at the foot of my bed had a cedar chest under it, and the horse blanket hung down almost to the chest. In my dream I was lying in bed, snuggled under the covers against the cold, when all the sudden, that particular horse blanket was eased back just a little as if by an unseen hand. Through that small space came a little red ball, one of those shiny red rubber balls about the size of a baseball.

"The ball bounced once off the top of the cedar chest, then bounced on the wooden floor. It bounced a few times on the floor, then rolled under the bed. In my dream I leaned over the side of the bed to find the ball, and that's when I suddenly woke up. As soon as my eyes opened I heard a noise in the kitchen. This was not normal. My grandmother didn't walk very well, especially on such a cold morning. I quickly got out of bed and rushed into the kitchen."

In the kitchen Catherine found her grandmother sitting in front of the stove with the oven door open. She had already turned on the four stovetop eyes and burned the paint off their metal covers, and she was trying to turn on the oven. If Catherine hadn't stopped her, it is quite possible the elderly woman could have been seriously injured or even burned down the house.

"My cousins and I often talk about how secure we felt in that house—as if we were being watched over," Catherine said. "I always thought it was our grandfather, somehow watching over the house he built and the woman he was married to for over sixty years. Whatever it was, I think it saved our lives that morning."

BOARDWALK

JOHNNY LEE GRISSOM AND ROGER HALL were not exactly impressionable teenagers. Both were well into their forties and both had families. It was a cold, frosty night and the two neighboring farmers were returning home from prayer service at the local church.

Johnny Lee was driving his pickup truck, and Butch, his dog, was riding in the back.

"Hey, Johnny Lee," said Roger, "look over there at the Newman place."

"Yeah, I see it. It's a light," said Johnny Lee, slowing the truck.

"But, there ain't nobody living in the Newman place," Roger said. "Besides, some feller from Knoxville bought it. Says he's going to fix it up for a vacation home."

"You're right. Let's go see what that light's all about."

As they drew closer, the pair could see a light moving from the barn toward the house. A wooden boardwalk about 150 feet in length ran from the barn to a side porch of the house. Johnny Lee and Roger climbed onto the planks to see who was walking up ahead.

"He's got a kerosene lantern," said Roger.

"Hush!" whispered Johnny Lee. "I think I hear something."

"Yeah, I can hear it, too. It sounds like footsteps. They're faint, but I can hear 'em."

"Oh, man," gasped Johnny Lee. "Do you see what I see?"

"Oh, my God," rasped Roger, "all I can see is two legs and the lantern."

"It must be the way the lantern's swinging," said Johnny Lee. "We just can't see the rest of him."

A chill settled over both men, then Roger called out, "Hey you, what are you doing here?"

There was no answer, only silence.

Johnny Lee put two fingers between his lips and whistled for the dog. "C'mon, Butch!" he yelled. "C'mon, Butch, sic him!"

The big hound leaped out of the truck and raced up the boardwalk. He passed Johnny Lee and Roger, then stopped abruptly and began to whimper.

The men glanced at each other, then dashed toward the house. But before they could close the distance, the lantern went out and the two mysterious legs, which had almost reached the side porch, disappeared.

Johnny Lee groped his way back to the truck and got a flashlight. Butch, tail between his legs, crawled toward the vehicle and jumped in the back, where he cowered in a corner.

"Let's check the doors," said Johnny Lee, thumbing the flashlight's switch. "Maybe that feller went inside."

The two checked all the entryways, but each was securely locked. They then forced open the kitchen door but found nothing, not even a kerosene lantern.

Shaking their heads in disbelief, they walked back to the truck and drove to Johnny Lee's place to call the sheriff. When the lawman arrived, he discovered three sets of footprints in the dust covering the boardwalk. Two sets belonged to Johnny Lee and Roger, but the third had been made by someone—or something—else.

"You know, Roger," said Johnny Lee, "I think we ought to forget about those legs and that lantern. Folks will think we've been chugging moonshine."

"Yeah," agreed Roger, "I think we'd best forget it. But I don't think old Butch is going to be able to. He still looks scared out of his wits!"

THE HERMIT'S WING

THE HOUSE WAS WELL OVER A HUNDRED years old, with gingerbread cornice work on the tall columns of the wraparound porch on the first floor. It had been magnificent in its day and later stood as a landmark in the lower reaches of the Georgia mountains.

Grady Banks had been born there, and eighty-three years later, he died there. The house and acreage were left to John, a grandson, and for the first time in his adult life, John could see a way to maybe make some money. He could envision the house divided into two apartments. It was surely large enough, and having several entrances could be easily accomplished.

It was a good plan, but once the place was cleared of all the grandfather's possessions, the old house looked different. It took on a different demeanor. The hardwood floors were rotten and the ceilings sagged and dipped. Even the lights with their hang-down bulbs and pull chains were beyond repair. The water pipes banged and clanged when the faucets were turned on, and they dripped a steady stream of rusty brown water when turned off.

After much time, money, and effort were expended, one side of the old house was ready to rent. Connie Gaddis, a young woman in her early twenties who was ready to step into life on her own, hurried to rent the apartment, even though renovations were still being made to the other side of the house.

With little to move, Connie was settled into the apartment in one day. She found the old house to be eerie, yet full of character, with cabinets reaching from floors to ceilings and fireplaces in every room.

Strange things began to happen on her second day there.

"Every time I closed a door, it opened as soon as my back was turned," Connie said. "And the same with the lights; I would turn them on and when I would start for the door, they would turn off.

"Sometimes I would hear voices—well, really just one. It was old and deep and scratchy, and it appeared to be reciting or reading aloud from Shakespeare.

"I never saw anything, but I always felt like an intruder in the house. I always believed something didn't want me to be there.

"I asked John, my landlord, about Mr. Banks, his grandfather. He didn't say much, just that Mr. Banks was a reclusive old man and didn't like anybody and discouraged the family from ever coming around. He said the family was a nuisance, just there to leech off him, and he didn't want to be bothered.

"It was the other side of the house that was really strange. That was where the grandfather lived during the last few years of his life. He had closed up the side I lived in. From what I can understand, Mr. Banks, or his spirit, made it perfectly clear he didn't want anybody there anytime on the side where he lived. Seems every time workers got something finished, it broke, or the workers' tools tore up or an accident happened.

"Actually, three different construction crews were hired and quit in the six months I lived there. Nobody would stay. Even in the heat of summer, the workers said the place was cold and their equipment wouldn't work most of the time.

"When dishes began breaking in the middle of the night on my side of the house, I moved in with a friend," said Connie in a trembling voice.

"I lived in Jefferson for about two more years, and when I left, the old house still stood empty and the renovations had never been completed.

"I guess the old man liked things just the way they were. He liked being left alone in life, and if everyone would leave him and his house alone in death, maybe he would rest in peace."

JOSIE'S GHOST

THE FAMILY REUNION IS THE SOCIAL EVENT of the year for the Wilkens clan. One year, because the autumn weather was so mild, the family decided to hold the reunion on the weekend of Halloween. About sixty Wilkenses attended, including twenty or so rambunctious children who were screaming for some fun. Finally, Janie Wilkens said she would tell a story about Aunt Josie's ghost.

Aunt Josie always said that not all ghosts are mean-spirited. Back then we all lived in the old homeplace. It wasn't much, just a big old three-story house with an attic. Now Josie—she was the one with the imagination—came down from the attic one suppertime and said, "We got a ghost, and he lives in the attic."

Most of us kids laughed and teased Josie. Someone, I think it was Uncle Ed, asked, "How come none of us never has seen any ghost? We all been up in the attic a thousand times."

"Yeah," we all screamed. "There isn't any ghost up there."

After about a month of kidding about her ghost, Josie informed us she would never mention it again.

One time, not long after that, we kids all sneaked up to the attic, and we heard Josie talking to someone. And the person she was talking to would answer her back. We burst through the door, and to our surprise, we saw only Josie. She was sitting on the floor looking at an old photo album.

"Who were you talking to?" demanded Marge.

"No one," smiled Josie as she continued to turn the pages of the album.

The years passed and we all forgot Josie's ghost. But you all know Josie never married. And she was so beautiful.

"This has been a great family reunion," Claudia said as Janie concluded her story about Josie, "but the kids are getting restless. We need some more ghost stories, anything. I don't know about anyone else's kids, but mine are driving me crazy."

"I know a little more about Josie and her ghost," said Uncle Ed. And with that, everyone gathered around as Ed began to tell what he knew of Josie's ghost.

It was the day Josie died. She was still living in the old place and had invited some children over for a Halloween party. She had candy corn, and kids dunked for apples. They all had a great time, and then the kids insisted on some ghost stories. Josie smiled and agreed, and she had told three or four when she got a funny look on her face. She told the kids that they'd have to go up to the attic for the next story. I was the only adult there except Josie.

"You see," Josie began, when she had joined the children in the attic, "some ghosts are shy. They never show themselves to people. Now, we've all heard tales about people being murdered and coming back to haunt the place they were slain in."

Josie paused and a strange look came over her face. I asked if she was all right, and she nodded. But I wasn't too sure about that; she looked different.

"Love or a broken heart," Josie continued, "can lead to a ghostly presence, but . . . " and here Josie faltered. She stood and smiled, and she looked as young and beautiful as she once was.

I tried to get to her—I knew then that Josie was ill—but she walked to the far corner of the attic. I knew it was crazy, but she looked like a young belle. The kids didn't seem to notice anything unusual, but I got a chill up and down my spine. I knew I was in the presence of something eerie.

Josie turned to me and with a stunning smile said, "Good-bye, Ed." And she fell to the attic floor.

I remember that at the funeral three days later, I told Granny the story of Josie's passing. And Granny, God bless her, said it best. She said, "Josie finally will be happy. She's with the person she loved for so many years, whoever he was."

Then Granny smiled that little smile of hers, and added, "We didn't bury Josie today. We just buried her body. This is what she's been waiting for all her life."

Perfume and Footsteps

"I USED TO HEAR MY FATHER'S FOOTSTEPS," Sherry said, a worried smile tugging at her lips. "And once, after I came back from a trip to Savannah, I heard his voice."

When we speak of ghostly doings in these modern times we automatically expect people won't believe our stories. Years ago talk of such things was more commonplace. Folks in the southern mountains spent hours relating such tales, and they were believed by almost everyone. But today talk of ghosts and spirits is something better done in the company of just a few close friends who share the same beliefs.

"You see," Sherry continued, "my father died unexpectedly. He was only in his mid-sixties, and despite bypass surgery the July before he died, we all expected he'd do just fine. So his death was really a shock to all of us. Our mother always seemed more fragile than Daddy, and I think he thought he'd outlive her. But he didn't. He had a massive heart attack about four months after his surgery and he died, leaving Mama alone."

Sherry looked out the double garden doors to the leaf-strewn patio beyond. Autumn had taken hold of the mountains and painted them with bold reds and yellows and golds. It was a time for drawing in, for quiet thought, for reflection.

"It was in April, after he died. Mama and I went to Savannah to visit Daddy's sisters. We had a really good time. One of Mama's sisters went with us and you couldn't ask for a better traveling companion.

"Anyway, when we got back, I was unloading the car, and that's when I heard Daddy's voice. He said, 'Y'all come on in.' I heard it as plain as day. I could just see him in my mind's eye, standing at the open screen door, saying, 'Y'all come on in.' After that I began to hear his footsteps inside the house.

"I lived with Mama then and worked during the day, but there came a time when she needed me at home because she was so ill that someone had to take care of her. That's when I started hearing his footsteps. Every time I'd step out onto the deck or be out in the yard near the house, I'd hear what I'll swear to you was him walking in the house. He had a very distinctive walk. He walked on the heels of his feet. His mother walked like that, his oldest sister walks like that, my oldest sister walks the same way, and so does her daughter. You could call it a family trait. Anyway, I could hear him walking through the house as plain as day."

This seemed to amuse Sherry. She laughed and the mood in the room lightened. She was no longer so sad while talking about her father.

"Once, Mama was in the hospital for an extended stay. I was in the house alone that entire time. I never saw anything but I certainly smelled something."

Sherry paused to sip her Earl Grey tea and let this part of the story settle in.

"About the second week Mama was in the hospital I began to notice a strange smell in her bedroom. It's hard to describe. The only thing I can liken it to is really expensive, really bad-smelling perfume. Just the kind of overwhelming perfume Daddy especially hated. He'd buy Mama Chanel for special occasions, birthdays and anniversaries, but that was it. He couldn't stand those heavy musks that seemed so popular in the eighties. So it was really strange that Mama's bedroom, the bedroom they shared, should smell just like the kind of perfume Daddy especially disliked.

"When I smelled the perfume in their room, I'd try to hunt down its source. I thought maybe someone had spilled some years ago and the scent only came out at certain times. But I could never pin it down to a particular spot in the room. I'd go hunting for it and the smell would just fade away to nothing. After Mama came home from the hospital I only smelled the perfume once more.

"The next few months Mama's health was pretty good. She went into the hospital again in February for a brief time. I was in the house alone for a few days. That's when I noticed a reoccurrence of that perfume smell.

"In April of that same year Mama went into the hospital for the last time. This time while she was gone, there were no unexplainable smells, no voices, no footsteps. In fact, the house seemed unusually quiet, as if it was waiting for something. Just a few days after Mama went into the hospital, that 'something' happened: Mama died."

Sherry became quiet for a moment. She held her tea mug and stared out at the perfect autumn day for a while before she finally continued.

"From the moment I walked into the house the afternoon after she died, I knew the house was different. It was as if only the living occupied the house. Later, when I was completely alone, I felt for the first time that I was truly alone. I didn't smell anything or hear anything. The house was still. No more perfume, no more footsteps.

"That's when I knew my father was finally gone. He no longer felt he had to take care of my mother. He could finally rest. They were both at peace. Together."

Sherry looked out the door, took a sip of tea, and sighed. She, too, was at peace.

BILLY'S REVENGE

BILLY WALDREN, A HULKING YOUTH, WAS considered by some to be a misfit. Some folks in Fannin County, Georgia, said he was kind of slow. Billy didn't go to school very often, but he did learn to read, and read quite well. Billy could fix just about anything. He'd take apart whatever it was and fix it.

Billy lived in a small cabin up in a hollow. The property was left to him by a great-aunt. He grew vegetables and had some chickens. Most of the locals would take their broken farm equipment or household appliances to Billy, and he would fix them. So all in all, Billy got along pretty well.

If there was a cloud over Billy's head, it was a fear of witches. Where he got that fear, no one knew, but it was a real fear to Billy. The young blades in town would tease Billy, saying things like, "See that lady over there? She's a witch."

When hearing that, Billy would run home to his cabin and lock himself in. Whenever he went into town, somebody would point out a lady as a witch.

One day Billy fixed a washing machine for a young couple that had just moved into an old farmhouse.

The wife asked, "Billy, do you know anybody who would want these old magazines? Some are at least ten years old. They go back to 1929."

Most were pulp magazines: adventure, mystery, science fiction, suspense, and horror.

"I'll take them, ma'am," said Billy, who took the magazines home and spent every free moment reading them.

It was an item in a horror pulp that saved his sanity. He read the passage, read it again, thought about it, then read it again.

"Gee," Billy said, "I don't have to worry about them old witches anymore. Just let them try something!"

One day late in October 1939 when Billy went to town, he met three young men.

"Say, Billy," asked one whose name was Ted. "How about going to a party with us?"

"Yes," said another named Jack. "It's a Halloween party. But you don't have to get dressed up. Just wear your regular clothes. We are."

"Why, thank you," said Billy, "I'd be proud to go with you. Where shall I meet you?"

"Right here at the feed store. How about seven o'clock?" said Ted.

Billy went home and got out the pulp magazine. He read the passage twice to make sure he had it right, then got ready to go to the party. Before he left, Billy went to the chest of drawers and took out a cigar box. It held a couple of tintypes of his grandparents, the deed to the property, and one other item, which, with a smile on his face, he put in his pocket.

Billy met Ted, Jack, and Lew at the feed store. "Everybody ready?" Ted asked. Everyone nodded and all four got into Ted's car, a 1938 four-door Chevrolet sedan. Actually, the car belonged to Ted's father, who was the county commissioner. They headed east, out of town.

"How far is it?" asked Billy.

"Not far now," answered Ted. "About another mile or so."

It was a moonless night, pitch dark, as they drove up a dirt road, at the end of which was an old shack owned by an ancient woman named Miss Parry. No one knew much about her; she was so old that she had outlived her contemporaries, and she had no kinfolk left. Some said she was a witch, but there was no proof of that because Miss Parry never bothered with anyone, and nobody ever, ever bothered with her.

Ted stopped the Chevrolet, and they all stepped out into the dark night.

"What is this place?" asked Billy. "Don't look like anybody else is here."

"They're all inside," said Jack. "Come on, we don't want to miss anything."

The four walked onto the small porch of the cabin, which looked like a good wind could blow over. Ted opened the door, and the other two pushed Billy inside. Then they followed him in.

"What do you want?" screeched Miss Parry, who certainly looked like a witch. She appeared to be at least a hundred years old, was small, hunched over, and had a hooked nose. Her eyes glistened with fury.

"Hey, you old witch!" yelled Ted. "Here's someone who wants to meet you. Maybe you can put a spell on him!" The three young men roared with laughter. Billy, who was closest to Miss Parry, was petrified with fright.

"So you want a spell, heh?" yelled the old woman. "Well, I got something special for you, my boy." Then she screamed a curse and ran right at Billy.

Billy, remembering the passage in the pulp magazine, reached in his pocket and pulled out what he had taken from the cigar box—a solid piece of silver, which he put in his mouth.

The old crone stopped, then backed away from Billy. She scrunched further back into the cabin, chanting something in a foreign tongue. Billy calmly walked out of the cabin and down the dirt road.

With Billy and his silver gone, Miss Parry shouted curses at the other young men.

"You three will have an accident. I curse you! You will have it before the clock strikes twelve midnight."

Ted, Jack, and Lew ran outside, jumped into the car, and sped down the dirt road. They passed Billy without even slowing.

Billy smiled as he remembered the passage in the pulp horror tale: "The only sure protection against a witch is a piece of silver. Just put it in your mouth, and the witch is helpless to do anything to you."

Billy reached the main road, started walking, and eventually was able to hitch a ride home.

When Billy went to town about a week later, he read the news in the local paper: The commissioner's son, Ted, along with the sheriff's son, Lew, and the preacher's son, Jack, had been involved in an accident. The three were not hurt too badly, but the commissioner's Chevrolet had been completely destroyed.

Billy reached into his pocket and felt the piece of silver. "Thank you," he said. "And I guess maybe Miss Parry really is a witch!"

Red Clay Bank

It WAS AN OLD RED CLAY BANK alongside the road. Nothing out of the ordinary to look at—just one of countless embankments that stood like ancient monoliths beside southern Appalachia's winding single-lane roadways. But something ordinary was not what Elizabeth Cooper saw when she passed it.

Elizabeth, a middle-aged woman who had lived her entire life in Raven County, didn't know how to explain what she saw there in the dirt, so she just said nothing.

She passed the place almost once a week on her way into town to buy groceries or pay bills. As the years passed, the bank began to give way and the clay slid onto the road. Before long, workers with earth-moving equipment came and began to shove the dirt back away from the road.

Drivers were pleased that somebody was taking responsibility, and people talked about the roadwork going on "up her way" when Elizabeth saw them in town and stopped to exchange pleasantries.

Elizabeth could still see something or feel it or know it when she passed the place, even though the bank itself was falling back.

"It's just dirt," she said aloud once when she passed the bulldozers that were pushing and pulling blades of the red clay to form terraces. But as the words mixed with the rumble of her old car's engine and then died away, a shiver of cold grabbed her and she shook with the chill.

Elizabeth was still trembling when she arrived home. She didn't know why but understood that it was somehow connected to the red clay bank beside the road.

One afternoon sometime later, Elizabeth and her husband, Cleve, passed the site on their way into town. It had stormed earlier in the day and the small mountain creeks and branches were overflowing, and the river that ran behind a field on the other side of the road from the bank ran high and red from backwaters.

Elizabeth took notice, then turned her attention from the raging waters to the bank. Rain had cut gullies down its face, and it appeared to be laughing streams of tears.

"It's a bad place here," she said aloud.

"Where?" asked Cleve as he steered the car carefully along the water-filled road.

"Here. No, I mean the bank," she answered, wishing that she had kept her feelings to herself.

"How do you mean, bad?" her husband asked. "Dangerous?"

"Maybe," she said. "I don't know. Something about the bank. Something's going to happen."

"What?" Cleve questioned, seeing the strange far-away look on Elizabeth's face.

"I don't know. But something connected to this spot of red clay bank is going to happen. And it's going to be bad," she responded.

The woman quickly changed the subject. She couldn't explain her feelings to herself, let alone explain them to anyone else.

Three weeks later, the owner of that spot of ground

was killed in an automobile accident and his two children were critically injured—one disabled for life.

Elizabeth was saddened by the news, but somehow she wasn't shocked by the event.

DOVE

YOU MAY HUNT THE HILLS OF SOUTHERN Appalachia and never see another living soul. Or do you? One morning Wallis Tynan and his sons walked out into their fog-shrouded pasture to do a little hunting before breakfast. It was like any other morning in spring. Wallis and his sons expected nothing unusual to happen, and they had a successful time of it until one of the hunters shot a dove.

By then the fog had cleared and the sky was a beautiful blue. The men knew the dove had been shot; they'd seen it fall. And, most strangely of all, the man who shot it saw a single downy feather float toward him on the breeze, then slide down the barrel of his gun and come to rest against his flushed cheek.

But no one could find the bird. Since they already had enough doves to make a good meal, Wallis decided it was time they headed home.

The rest of day as they went about their chores, the men thought little of the lost dove. There was much to do on the farm, and the sun set too early to accomplish everything. By evening they were well and truly worn out, and ready for supper and bed.

Supper was hearty fare: rabbit and squirrel, fried chicken and ham, biscuits and cornbread, snap beans, boiled cabbage, potato patties, and for dessert, sweet potatoes with fresh butter. But when the family sat down at the kitchen table, their meal was interrupted by a noise at the front door.

Wallis sent one of his sons to see what was causing the noise, with strict instructions to invite whoever was at the front door to come in and sit down to supper. When the son returned, his face was pale and drawn, and he motioned for his father to come to the door. Wallis did so at once.

When Wallis got to the front door, he found it standing open. His son told him to look outside on the porch, and Wallis did so without hesitation. After a moment, he could not believe his eyes and called to the rest of the family to come and see for themselves.

On the porch was a dove, which had been tapping on the door with its beak. Wallis knew immediately that it was the same dove one of his sons had shot that morning. He knew that was true because the dove's wing was broken and it had trailed blood across the porch.

Anxious to help the bird, Wallis stooped and scooped it into his hands. He held the dove close and stroked its breast and tried to see if the damage to the wing was serious. That was when he noticed that the bird lay stiff and cold in his hands—as if it had been dead a long time rather than mere minutes.

He didn't want to tell his family, especially the younger ones, that the dove was so oddly cold, so he pretended that it had died while he held it. But when Wallis handed the bird to the son who had shot it, the son noted the condition of the dove and told his brothers about it later.

For years Wallis would neither confirm nor deny that the bird had been dead for hours before it came tapping on the door. He merely said it was odd that, of all the porches in the area, the dove had come onto the Tynans' porch. Also, he refused to hunt doves after the incident, and no one in the Tynan family would either, not to this day. Rabbits, squirrels, and even deer, but never, ever doves.

THE PURPLE CLOUD

RELIGION IS A STRONG FORCE IN SOUTHERN Appalachia, and in years past—and perhaps even today—parents and their children prayed together several times each day. People prayed to build faith, give thanks, and ask for divine guidance in a time when life was hard at best. Such was the case of a young man named Doug.

Doug is a soft-spoken man who lives a secluded life against a mountain in the far reaches of Gilmer County, Georgia. He works out of his hundred-year-old house with its uneven floors and hang-down lights with pull chains. A computer genius who does repair work for little above cost, Doug also tutors, donating much time and effort to children needing extra help with their learning skills. He occasionally scrapes together a computer for children who can't afford one, helping to bring them into today's computer world.

"I'll never get rich," he says. "But, I'm content to have my needs simply met."

When asked about any ghostly hauntings or strange experiences in his old house or his life, Doug hesitated. Then, giving a gentle nod of his head, he told the following story of a nighttime visitor from his childhood.

"We didn't speak of such things in my family," Doug said. "We were very religious, praying several times a day, and to speak of anything unusual could be construed as speaking of something unholy or satanic, as I discovered when I was about seven years old.

"It was a little purple cloud. It hovered above the foot of my bed every night. I didn't think it was strange or unusual, maybe because it had always been there. Then I spoke to Libby, my sister, about it.

"She had no cloud above her bed, nor could she see the one in my room.

"'There,' I said, pointing one night when I had convinced her it was really there and she should come and see it. 'See, it's just a little purple cloud.'

"'You're making this up. There's nothing there,' Libby huffed. 'I'm going to tell Daddy you're telling fibs.'

"'No, Libby, I'm not. Just look. Can't you see it?' I asked, wondering why my sister was denying the cloud was there.

"'There's nothing there, Doug,' Libby said as she stomped out of the bedroom. 'And I think you're being mean to play tricks on me.'

"I didn't say anything else about the cloud for a while, but took comfort that it was indeed there and perhaps was a nighttime guardian."

Time passed and Doug again broached the subject of the purple cloud. But this time he spoke to his parents. Both went to his room to investigate and saw nothing even though the boy insisted it was there.

After much discussion, Doug was discouraged from ever speaking of the cloud again.

"It could be evil," said his father, a preacher of long service and good standing in the community. "If your mother and I can't see it, it's just not there. Do you understand? We want you to pray every morning and every night and ask God to forgive your sins because you've obviously stirred up some kind of evil and Satan is after you. The rest of us will pray, too."

Doug cringed, knowing he would not deliberately stir up evil and definitely didn't want the devil lurking about trying to get him. He agreed to his parents' demands. He also agreed never to mention the purple cloud to anyone again. Yet, it remained a nighttime companion and emanated a warm, comfortable feeling just hovering above his bed while he slept.

The cloud stayed with Doug, even though the family moved to several different small communities in the low-lying foothills as Doug's father went where the calling took him and the need for ministering the gospel was greatest.

The cloud was there each night when sleep took him, until Doug became a young adult and grew somewhat rowdy and rebellious. He can't recall exactly when he stopped seeing the little cloud, he just realized one night that it was gone.

"And, now," he says, "I've grown up, matured, and left the rabble-rousing far behind. I don't ever see the little purple cloud hovering at the foot of my bed before I go to sleep. But I often feel its presence. I know it's still there and that it's not evil but a goodness of some kind, giving me the feeling of a warm hug whenever I feel cold."

The Keepers of the White Dog

For generations superstitions have been a large part of everyday life in the Appalachian foothills. Many of the old superstitions have been lost over time, but Miss Ibee Taylor remembers her family talking about the white dog. Miss Ibee, who is well into her eighties but possesses a bright, clear mind, states that many of the old superstitions came from the Cherokees and that many of the local folk had ancestors who were Native Americans. Miss Ibee says the white dog phenomenon came from her Cherokee people, and the white dog was originally a pure white wolf.

Back in the early part of the twentieth century, Ibee's grandparents lived up on a ridge. One day Jonas Taylor, her grandfather, stepped out onto the porch of his cabin and saw, standing about a hundred feet away between the wagon ruts in the dirt road, a large white dog.

"Come here, boy!" yelled Jonas. "Come on, come here!" But the animal ignored him. Jonas walked toward the white dog, but it backed away and Jonas could get no closer than when he first saw the dog.

Ruth, Jonas's wife, came out and said, "That sure is a handsome dog. Wonder where he came from?"

Try as he might, Jonas could not coax the dog to come to him and finally he gave up. John and Ruth went on to church but, surprisingly, the dog followed them.

"Say, John," asked Jonas outside the church, "you don't know who that white dog belongs to, do you?"

John Delvin, a lumberman, turned and said, "No, I don't. But this is a fine-looking animal." The dog was large and powerful looking, with somewhat matted pure white fur.

Jonas asked several other men waiting outside the church, but this time he received different answers. "What white dog?" or "Ain't no dog there, white or otherwise!" or "Jonas, you been drinking shine?"

Jonas didn't understand what was happening. He, Ruth, and John Delvin all could see the dog plain as day. But no one else seemed to be able to see it.

Two days later they heard that John Delvin had been crushed to death when a wagonload of timber rolled over on him.

Neither Jonas nor Ruth saw the white dog for a month or so, then he showed up again. The dog just sat in the dirt road and ignored Jonas and Ruth, as if it was waiting for something—or someone.

Ruth called the family out to see the dog. And from six-year-old Henry to Grandpap, all the Taylors could see him.

The animal stayed two days, and when Jonas and Ruth went into town to get some staples, the white dog went with them. While Ruth went in the store, Jonas chatted with the men at the feed store.

"Where's that white dog of yours?" someone asked. "Yes, the dog no one can see." All the men laughed but one, Hike Watson. The dog stood across the street, just looking at the men.

After a bit, Hike said quietly to Jonas. "Jonas, I can see the dog. I don't know what's a matter with those fellows. It's right there across the street."

"I guess they're just trying to be funny," said Jonas. "It don't matter to me. All my kinfolk can see him and that is that. Only trouble is, I wish I could make friends with him, but I can't get near him."

A week later, Hike Watson, at age thirty-five, drowned in Miller's Pond—a pond barely four feet deep.

Although the white dog came to the Taylor place, and all of them could see him, no members of the family ever died in an accident. Sometimes the white dog would be gone for months, then would return and sit in front of the Taylors' home. Once, there were visitors, and two people saw the dog. They were killed when their wagon overturned.

As the years passed, Jonas and the rest of the Taylors never mentioned the white dog, even though he still showed up.

Miss Ibee was born in 1910, which made her the youngest, with Henry the next youngest.

"I never did see the white dog," she says, "but my grandparents, my great-aunts and -uncles, my parents, all swore they saw the dog. But after Henry died, there was no one else left in my family who saw the dog. I heard all the tales of the accidental deaths, and years later I heard of other families who had similar experiences.

"Superstition, mass hysteria, I don't know. But my kinfolk believed in the white dog. And when he showed up, and someone other than my family saw him, it meant somebody was going to die, usually in some terrible accident. And usually in the prime of their life."

THE OLD INNES PLACE

FLORA INNES TELLS ABOUT HER GREAT-grandparents' home back in the mountains not far from Murphy, North Carolina. Over the years so many Inneses passed away in the two-story log house that folks thought the place was haunted.

I was just a little girl, oh, about ten or eleven, and my parents took me up in the mountains to visit my grandparents. During the day we had a picnic, and we all had a fun time.

It was just before dusk when I saw an old woman walk out the living-room door onto the porch. I asked my grandmother who that old lady was. She smiled and said it was her aunt Edith.

"Stop that," Mama said. "You'll scare Flora." It seems Aunt Edith had died twenty years before.

I wasn't really scared. The woman looked so very old, I didn't think she could hurt me. Later, as we sat inside, I heard a noise out in the yard. I went to the window and looked out, and there was a young man standing in front of the log house. He wasn't doing anything, he was just standing there. I asked Grandpa who the young man was.

"Oh, that's Harley," Grandpa said. "He comes once or twice a week. 'Course he's been dead about forty years."

Now you must think we were all crazy, but I did see the old woman and someone who was supposed to be Harley Innes. I was young at the time, and maybe the tales I heard influenced me. Well, I don't know, but I did see two other people that weekend. I know I saw them and I was told they were long-ago ancestors.

It was Sunday afternoon and I was just walking along the creek bank, watching the water rush by. I must have slipped, because the next thing I knew, I was in the creek. I panicked because I couldn't swim, and even though the water wasn't deep, I couldn't get my footing. I kept falling back in the water, and it seemed to me I was being swept down the stream.

I tried to scream, but I went under and I swallowed water. I thought I was going to drown, when a hand reached down and grabbed my hair and pulled me out onto the bank.

When I opened my eyes, a boy sat next to me. I coughed and thanked him and I asked his name. He said his name was Jeeter and he was twelve years old. Finally I stood, and after thanking him again, I asked him to come back to my grandparents' house. He said he'd like to but he had to go.

I went back to the house, and Mama screamed when she saw me, all soaking wet. I think she thought I was a ghost, there being so much ghost talk during our stay there. I explained how I fell in the creek and how a nice boy pulled me out."

"Who was it pulled you out of the creek?" Grandmother asked.

"He said his name was Jeeter," I answered.

Well, you could have heard a pin drop. And I'll never forget what my grandfather said then.

"Jeeter! Well, I'll be darned. Jeeter Innes—he was my

cousin and he drowned in that creek fifty years ago. He was 12 years old at the time."

Of all the things that happened that weekend, including my almost drowning, I guess the scariest was—well, it's hard to explain but here goes: If you wanted to go into the kitchen, you had to go out the living room, across the porch, and put your hand through a hole in the kitchen door and lift a latch to open it. And nearly every time you did put your hand in the hole it felt like a hand would grab yours. It was a hand as cold as ice, and it would hold your hand for a moment, then let loose. I still think about this today, fifty years later.

To tell the truth, neither I nor my parents ever went back to that house. And every time I pass through Murphy, North Carolina, I get a chill and shivers down my back.

EPILOGUE

THERE HAVE BEEN MANY CHANGES IN THE southern Appalachian foothills since the first settlers arrived here. Most of them have occurred in the last dozen years, many in the last five. The interstate highway system is the main reason for the change. The foothills now boast—or are cursed with, depending on the point of view—many new housing developments and industries, and the pristine mountains no longer supply the frontier family with food. Now the birds are startled not by a lone hunter but by the sound of a golf club driving a small ball and by children shouting as they play in deep lakes that once supplied fish for mountain folks.

The interstates also brought shopping malls. Not too long ago folks would pack up the family and head for a larger town or city perhaps some seventy miles away—usually once a year at Christmas or occasionally for a wedding or funeral. The rest of the time folks shopped locally, and many, if not all, had large vegetable gardens. In the autumn the womenfolk would preserve the harvest by canning or drying the fruits and vegetables. Later, the local extension services would operate canneries for the locals, doing away with much of the drudgery of home food preservation. These canneries still operate in the fall in the foothills.

On Main Street or on the square, family-owned businesses sold furniture, hardware, and other necessities of life. Today most of these businesses are gone, the malls with their major department stores having tolled the death knell for most of them. Although many older businesses have gone under, the Main Streets are thriving once again. Where the local sweet shop or furniture store once did business, now gift shops, bookstores, and computer stores have taken their place. In one section of southern Appalachia, there are now more than a half-dozen bookstores. Three counties have built new libraries and others are being planned.

Many of these improvements could not have happened without an influx of new people. Many of these people dedicate countless hours to libraries, arts councils, historical societies, local hospitals, and civic organizations.

Many Appalachian people now have cable television, and their families rent movies in town to replay on their VCRs. Children—even schools—now have computers, and even dad finds ways to use the newfangled machine. Most folks still have their backyard gardens, and much produce is still preserved for use when supermarket prices get too high.

Two things, though, remain the same: church and legends. Come Sunday, in scores of churches the folks celebrate God with neighbors they have known since childhood. This area isn't called the Bible Belt for nothing.

Legends bring families together as the old mountain tales are told on rainy or snowy nights somewhere in the southern Appalachian foothills. Told by grandparents or great-aunts or -uncles, ghost stores still hold the children spellbound as they have for generations. Who can forget the chills and goose bumps of a ghost story told by a loving relative?

Still, many worry that with computers and VCRs, many of these stories and legends will be lost forever. This would be a terrible loss for generations yet to come. That's why even as modernization slowly works its way into rural areas, it is important that stories like these be preserved. It would be tragic if the old ways and the area's heritage were lost.